ALWāYS

D0167713

Books by Melody Carlson

ALWаYS

A TEEN DEVOTIONAL

Words from the Rock

MELODY CARLSON

Revell

a division of Baker Publishing Group
Grand Rapids, Michigan

© 2010 by Melody Carlson

Published by Revell
a division of Baker Publishing Group
P.O. Box 6287, Grand Rapids, MI 49516-6287
www.revellbooks.com

Printed in the United States of America

Library of Congress Cataloging-in-Publication Data
Carlson, Melody.
    Always : a teen devotional / Melody Carlson.
        p.   cm. — (Words from the Rock)
    ISBN 978-0-8007-3256-1 (pbk.)
    1. Christian teenagers—Prayers and devotions. 2. Bible. N.T. Gospels—
Meditations. I. Title.
BV4850.C3325 2010
242'.63—dc22   2010021024

In keeping with biblical principles of creation stewardship, Baker Publishing Group advocates the responsible use of our natural resources. As a member of the Green Press Initiative, our company uses recycled paper when possible. The text paper of this book is comprised of 30% postconsumer waste.

12   13   14   15   16   7   6   5   4   3   2

Contents

Introduction

*J*esus is the Rock, and a relationship with him will rock your world. At the age of fifteen, I did a major 180-degree turnaround when I went from devout atheist to Jesus freak. Hungry to find out more about God, I began to devour the Bible. I started in the New Testament and read and read. I memorized entire chapters. I participated in Bible study groups. I read books about the Bible. I attended conferences. It was like I couldn't get enough.

Then, many years later, I felt somewhat saturated by the Bible and Christian teaching and theology in general. I felt like someone who'd sat at Thanksgiving dinner too long—I was stuffed. So for a while, I went on a diet and abstained from reading. To be honest, I felt a little guilty about that. I mean, doesn't a "good" Christian read her Bible every day?

That's when I got a redlined Bible, in which all the words of Jesus are written in red ink so they stand out. I decided that's all I would read—just the red lines.

I quickly rediscovered that those words (Jesus's words) were packed with wisdom, truth, and life. And why wouldn't they be? So that's why I wanted to write a devotional series that primarily uses just the words of Jesus.

Always is the third and final book in this series (following *True* and *Life*). This devotional is special in that it features Scriptures from the last days of Jesus's earthly life—including some powerful prayers and strong words of encouragement. One of the major themes of Jesus's final teachings was the need to hold tightly to him. No matter what comes your way, Jesus wants you to stay linked to him. In the same way a branch clings to the trunk of the tree, to sustain life and grow fruit, Jesus wants you to cling to him. He wants you so connected that nothing—no storms, earthquakes, droughts—can shake you loose.

1

The Only Way

> *I am the way, and the truth, and the life. The only*
> *way to the Father is through me. If you really knew*
> *me, you would know my Father, too. But now you*
> *do know him, and you have seen him.*
>
> John 14:6–7 NCV

*S*ometimes it's hard to grasp how tightly connected Jesus and God are—so intricately intertwined that they are inseparable; they are one. Maybe you're wondering, if they are one, why do we need both? Basically it's because God wanted to get our attention and we weren't listening. In fact, the human race had kind of tuned God out.

To understand this better, imagine you're a beekeeper. Okay, it's a stretch, but just go with it. Now imagine you own the only beehive in the world, but you know that all your bees are going to be wiped out by a rare disease. Your bees make great honey, and you really love them and don't want them to die. If only they would listen to you, they could change some of their bee habits and survive. So you stand over their hive telling them over and over what they must do to prevent their doom, but they don't understand you. Or maybe they're not listening, or maybe they're as busy as bees and totally oblivious to any danger. How do you communicate to them? How do you keep them from perishing?

What if you became one of them? What if you had the power to transform yourself into a bee? Then you could go inside the hive and talk directly to the bees. Speaking Bee-glish, you could make them understand your concerns.

Now, as silly as this bee metaphor sounds, it's a bit like God's decision to send Jesus to earth. Jesus was part of God, and God knew that if he became one of us, he could get our attention. Jesus became God's ambassador, the way to connect us to God. So how connected do you feel? How much more connected would you like to be?

My Prayer

Dear God,
Help me to grasp that you and Jesus are one, and that you poured yourself into Jesus so you could pour yourself into me.
Amen.

Stone
for the Journey

God and Jesus are one, and they want to be one with me.

Final Word

For God so loved the world that he gave his one and only Son, that whoever believes in him shall not perish but have eternal life.

John 3:16 NIV

One and the Same

Words from the Rock

Anyone who has seen me has seen the Father! So why are you asking me to show him to you? Don't you believe that I am in the Father and the Father is in me? The words I speak are not my own, but my Father who lives in me does his work through me. Just believe that I am in the Father and the Father is in me. Or at least believe because of the work you have seen me do.

John 14:9–11 NLT

What do you think you'd do if you had only a week to live? Maybe your first response would be to do something crazy and reckless, like skydiving or bungee jumping or drag racing. Or maybe you'd go on some wild spending spree and live large. Or you might take some time to be alone to contemplate. But before long, you'd probably want to focus on people and relationships. You might need to tell someone you love them or that you're sorry, or you might need to forgive someone. You'd probably want to really talk to the ones you love the most—to speak openly and from the heart.

If you knew your days were numbered, you'd probably want to connect on a much deeper level with anyone who meant anything to you, especially with the people you truly love. You'd want to make sure that your friends and loved ones understood who you were and what mattered to you, and in the same way, you'd want to understand them. Most likely, you would want to leave this world knowing that your relationships were in super good shape.

The verses above are words Jesus speaks just days before his death. You can hear the urgency in his message. More than anything, he wants to be sure his loved ones really know him. He wants them to understand how tightly connected he is to God so that when he's gone, his followers will realize that their connection to God is because of Jesus. He wants them to know that it's a connection that cannot be broken.

Those words are spoken to you too. Jesus invites you—in the same way he invited his disciples—to become partners with him and his Father.

My Prayer

Dear God,
It's easy to take relationships for granted.
Please remind me of the importance of having
a good one with you, and how it impacts my
relationships with others.
Amen.

Stone
for the Journey

**I'm made
strong by my
relationship
with Jesus.**

Final Word

A body is made up of many parts, and each of them has its own use. That's how it is with us. There are many of us, but we each are part of the body of Christ, as well as part of one another.

Romans 12:4–5 CEV

3
Humble Entrances

Words from the Rock

*Go over to the village across from you. You'll find
a donkey tethered there, her colt with her. Untie
her and bring them to me. If anyone asks what
you're doing, say, "The Master needs them!" He
will send them with you.*

Matthew 21:2–3 Message

*N*ot long before Jesus dies, he makes a historical ride into
the city of Jerusalem. Now, remember that Jesus is the
Son of God (the same God who created and rules the universe), and
no mightier king has ever walked the earth. So how would a king of
this magnitude enter the religious capital of the world? Nowadays
an important ruler might arrive in a long motorcade of shiny limou-
sines, escorted by security and motorcycle police. In Jesus's time, a
powerful king might arrive on a majestic white stallion, surrounded
by his army, with trumpets and flags and fanfare.

Yet what does Jesus tell his disciples to bring for his ride into Jerusalem? A donkey. And not even a grown donkey, but the colt of a

donkey. Now keep in mind that, according to some historians, Jesus was taller than average, which means his legs were probably rather long. Can you picture a tall man riding on the back of a juvenile donkey, with his feet literally dragging on the ground? Does that sound like the way royalty usually travels? But long ago, prophets had predicted this very thing—that their king would arrive on a donkey's colt, and the people would recognize and welcome him. And they did.

Ironically, Jesus first entered the world as a helpless baby, born in a barn. Now he enters the city as a king riding on a baby donkey. Jesus arrives with an unexpected humility, yet he is the Son of God. For some reason this gets people's attention—a man with the power of the universe at his disposal who doesn't force his way.

Think about the quiet ways Jesus enters your life. Consider how you respond to his entrance. Do you welcome him?

My Prayer

Dear God,
Thank you for the way you humbly enter my life, and for the way you quietly change my heart when I welcome you in.
Amen.

Final Word

He is the image of the invisible God, the firstborn over all creation.

Colossians 1:15 NIV

Stone
for the Journey

Jesus makes a humble entrance with powerful results.

4

Earth-Shaking Faith

Words from the Rock

> *I tell you the truth, if you have faith and don't doubt, you can do things like this and much more. You can even say to this mountain, "May you be lifted up and thrown into the sea," and it will happen. You can pray for anything, and if you have faith, you will receive it.*
>
> Matthew 21:21–22 NLT

Short of a volcanic eruption unlike anything man has ever seen, or a nuclear explosion that would most likely end life as we know it, it's pretty hard to imagine how a mountain could be lifted and thrown into the sea. Furthermore, why would anyone want that to happen? If those mountain-moving events really did occur, the results would probably include some major global warming, not to mention a total meltdown of the polar icecaps. Really, why would anyone want to move a mountain? Unless that mountain was in the way.

In Jesus's time, most travel was done on foot. If there was a mountain between point A and point B, travelers would have to go around it. A mountain was an obstacle, an obstruction, a hindrance to commuting. It slowed people down. For that reason, there might have been times when a weary traveler would have liked to toss the mountain into the sea. Of course, that wasn't possible.

Maybe that's why Jesus uses the mountain-moving metaphor—because it sounds so impossible. Maybe Jesus wants us to grasp that when we have faith in him, we are able to do the impossible.

What is the mountain in your life? What is it that gets in your way, slows you down, and comes between where you are and where you want to be? Is it a tough relationship? An addiction? An inability to forgive someone? Those kinds of things are like mountains—they obstruct your way. Have you asked Jesus to give you the faith to move that mountain?

My Prayer

Dear God,
Please help me to recognize the mountains that need to be removed from my life. Give me the kind of earth-shaking faith to move them.
Amen.

Stone
for the Journey

With Jesus, I can remove mountains from my life.

Final Word

What then shall we say to these things?
If God is for us, who is against us?

Romans 8:31 NASB

Miracle Key

> *I tell you the truth, anyone who has faith in me will do what I have been doing. He will do even greater things than these, because I am going to the Father. And I will do whatever you ask in my name, so that the Son may bring glory to the Father. You may ask me for anything in my name, and I will do it.*
>
> John 14:12–14 NIV

*I*t's hard to imagine doing the kinds of amazing things Jesus did while he was on earth. For starters, Jesus performed miracles like feeding thousands of hungry people with a few loaves of bread. He restored vision to blind people, healed lame people, and cast out real live demons. He was able to walk on the water in the middle of the sea. He could stop a hurricane with the sound of his voice. He even raised the dead. Seriously, those are some pretty big sandals to try to fill. Yet Jesus tells us we can do even greater things. How is that even possible?

Perhaps we should start with our measuring tools. How do you gauge what's greater or better or more amazing when it comes to miracles? Don't you think the blind man (who received his vision) would have argued with the hungry person (who ate the loaves and fishes) that his eyesight miracle was superior? And what about the time Jesus helped Peter to walk on the water instead of drown? Wouldn't Peter think that was a pretty great miracle?

Maybe miracles are relative. Maybe it's the miracles each of us needs the most that are the greatest. For instance, what if you really want to tell a friend about how cool it is to have a relationship with God, but you get so nervous that you're always tongue-tied when you want to bring it up? But let's say you prayed and asked God to help you, and the next thing you know, you're sitting there telling your friend all about God. Wouldn't that seem like a pretty huge miracle?

Jesus is the key that opens the door to a miracle. Why not start asking for him to help you with some miracles in your life? Remember, with God anything is possible.

My Prayer

Dear God,
I want to believe that you can do some amazing miracles in my life. Show me some of the things you want to do, and remind me to ask for your help.
Amen.

Stone
for the Journey

With Jesus I can do some miraculous things.

Final Word

God began doing a good work in you, and I am sure he will continue it until it is finished when Jesus Christ comes again.

Philippians 1:6 NCV

6

On Second Thought

Words from the Rock

What do you think? There was a man who had two sons. He went to the first and said, "Son, go and work today in the vineyard."

"I will not," he answered, but later he changed his mind and went.

Then the father went to the other son and said the same thing. He answered, "I will, sir," but he did not go.

Which of the two did what his father wanted?

Matthew 21:28–31 NIV

*S*ometimes it seems easier to say yes and agree to something you really don't want to do simply to avoid conflict or to impress someone. Imagine that a youth group leader is asking for volunteers at the soup kitchen next weekend. Jenny Doe doesn't want to appear to be the selfish kind of person who'd rather sleep in on Saturday, so she smiles and politely raises her hand. That way she looks good. But even as her hand is up, she's planning a way to conveniently forget all about this commitment, or maybe she'll neglect to set her alarm clock, or maybe she'll fabricate some other believable excuse like a case of the twenty-four-hour flu. The point is, she wants to look good.

There's a word for someone like that—*hypocrite*, or, as many were called in Jesus's day, *religious leaders*. Unfortunately, a lot of the most seemingly religious people were big fat hypocrites. When Jesus told this story, he was trying to make his listeners understand that the religious hypocrites were the ones pretending to serve God and others, but when no one was looking, they were serving only themselves. Like the son who says, "Yes, Dad," but fully intends to break that promise, the hypocrites could not be trusted.

What about the son who says, "No way, Dad," but later changes his mind and does what he's been asked? He represents the person who has rebelled against God—someone who's broken the rules— but later realizes his mistake and wants to change. Those are the kinds of people Jesus is looking for. People who recognize they're sinners but want to turn their lives around. Jesus can work with people like that.

So are you a yes person who secretly means no? Or are you a no person who, after a change of heart, wants to say yes to God?

My Prayer

Dear God,
I know I've made mistakes and I've broken some promises. I'm sorry, and I want to live my life the way you want me to. Please help me to do that. Amen.

Stone
for the Journey

With Jesus's help, I will keep my promises to God.

Final Word

You were rescued by the precious blood of Christ, that spotless and innocent lamb.

1 Peter 1:19 CEV

7

Our Helper

If you love me, you will do as I command. Then I will ask the Father to send you the Holy Spirit who will help you and always be with you. The Spirit will show you what is true. The people of this world cannot accept the Spirit, because they don't see or know him. But you know the Spirit, who is with you and will keep on living in you.

John 14:15–17 CEV

What if you were suddenly transplanted into a completely different country—someplace where everything was totally foreign to you? What if you couldn't speak the language and your money was no good? Plus your clothes were all wrong, you were completely lost, you didn't know a single soul, and there was no American embassy. What would you do? Forget any hopes of enjoying your stay there, but can you think of anything that might make your visit a little less miserable?

How about a guide? What if a friendly local, someone who knew the area and language and could speak English, stepped up and offered you a helping hand? Wouldn't that be a huge relief?

Jesus knew that our spiritual journey wasn't going to be easy. In some ways, it would be like traveling through a foreign country. Jesus understood we would need some help to navigate our way. That's why he sent an invisible piece of himself to live inside of us. Whether we call this the Holy Spirit, our helper, our counselor, or even our personal guide, it is Jesus's Spirit living inside of us—and it's available to everyone who loves Jesus and believes in him.

But this Spirit can help us only when we let him. Remember the guide in the foreign country? What if he warned you not to go into a treacherous neighborhood or eat a lethal food, but you refused to listen? The outcome could be fatal. Similarly, Jesus gives you his Spirit to whisper truth to your heart, to gently guide you away from danger—but if you don't listen, you will get hurt.

My Prayer

Dear God,
I want your Spirit to live inside me. Help me to tune in to his quiet voice, heed his advice, and obey.
Amen.

Stone
for the Journey

Jesus's Spirit can guide me through anything.

Final Word

If the Spirit of him who raised Jesus from the dead is living in you, he who raised Christ from the dead will also give life to your mortal bodies through his Spirit, who lives in you.

Romans 8:11 NIV

8

Messes Welcome

Words from the Rock

> *I tell you the truth, the tax collectors and the pros-*
> *titutes are entering the kingdom of God ahead of*
> *you. For John came to you to show you the way of*
> *righteousness, and you did not believe him, but*
> *the tax collectors and the prostitutes did. And*
> *even after you saw this, you did not repent and*
> *believe him.*
>
> Matthew 21:31–32 NIV

*C*an you picture the expressions on the faces of the religious leaders when Jesus targeted them with these strong words? Keep in mind that the religious leaders did everything possible to *look* good—they went out of their way to keep up the appearance of being holy and pure and spiritually superior to everyone else. Now Jesus was telling them that the lowlifes—the ones they considered to be the bottom-feeders of society—were going to make it into heaven ahead of them! They must have been seriously annoyed.

In that culture, no one was considered more messed up than prostitutes and tax collectors—prostitutes for obvious reasons, and tax collectors because they were considered "legalized" thieves. Jesus was declaring that messed-up people like that were actually going to heaven? How was that possible? Yet Jesus made it clear why messy lives would be welcome in heaven—it was because they welcomed the message that both John the Baptist and Jesus had shared with them. They admitted that they'd been caught in a corrupt lifestyle and wanted to change. They received Jesus's forgiveness and became believers. Of course they would be welcome in heaven.

In the meantime, most of the religious leaders refused to admit to their own shortcomings. They were trapped by their own pride and arrogance, and their biggest concern was to keep up the facade that they were better than everyone else.

Hiding our messes beneath a cloak of religion or fake goodness is always a mistake—it's like living a lie. Jesus encourages us to own up to our faults, to admit to our failures. And just as we welcome his forgiveness, he welcomes us into heaven!

My Prayer

Dear God,
Thank you for showing me that my life is messy. Give me strength to confess my problems to you so that you can forgive me and help me to get past them.
Amen.

Stone
for the Journey

When I confess
to my mess,
Jesus can
clean me up.

Final Word

If we confess our sins, he is faithful and just and will forgive us our sins and purify us from all unrighteousness.

1 John 1:9 NIV

9

Never Alone

Words from the Rock

No, I will not abandon you as orphans—I will come to you. Soon the world will no longer see me, but you will see me. Since I live, you also will live. When I am raised to life again, you will know that I am in my Father, and you are in me, and I am in you.

John 14:18–20 NLT

One of the greatest fears of small children is to lose their parents. Whether it be through death, abandonment, kidnapping, or whatever, young children do not want to be left parentless. Of course, this changes as kids grow older, and some teenagers might even act like they'd be perfectly fine without any parental influence. Although they probably know deep down that they still need a safe place to live and someone to watch out for them.

But what if the stakes are much higher for children than simply being sure that they'll have a roof over their heads, food on the table, and clothes to wear? What if the stakes are life and death . . . heaven and hell? That's what Jesus is talking about. He knows that his earthly life is about to end and that his disciples will feel like lost children when he's taken from them. Sure, they may be grown men and able to care for themselves when it comes to their earthly needs, but what about their spiritual needs? By now they know and respect Jesus as the Son of God. They understand that he is living water to their thirsty souls, the bread of life for their deepest hunger, and the key to the kingdom of heaven. What will they do without him?

Jesus assures his disciples that even though it might appear he's gone, he's not. He promises to show himself to them—and to us. He promises that he'll always be a part of us and we'll always be a part of him. We will never be spiritual orphans; we will never be abandoned. He will always be there, ready to provide for our spiritual necessities. That's his promise, and we can hold on to it until the end of time.

My Prayer

Dear God,
Thank you for the promise that you will never leave or abandon me. Please remind me of that when I feel lonely—remind me that you're still with me.
Amen.

Stone
for the Journey

Jesus will never abandon me.

Final Word

Christ gives meaning to your life, and when he appears, you will also appear with him in glory.

Colossians 3:4 CEV

10

Mismanagement

> *There was a landowner who planted a vineyard.*
> *. . . He rented the vineyard to some farmers and*
> *went away on a journey. When the harvest time*
> *approached, he sent his servants to the tenants*
> *to collect his fruit.*
>
> *The tenants seized his servants; they beat one,*
> *killed another, and stoned a third. Then he sent*
> *other servants to them . . . and the tenants treated*
> *them the same way. Last of all, he sent his son to*
> *them. "They will respect my son," he said.*
>
> *But when the tenants saw the son, they . . .*
> *threw him out of the vineyard and killed him.*
>
> Matthew 21:33–39 NIV

One of the most aggravating stories to make the news—and unfortunately it seems to happen too much—is when some mega-corporation, high-up executive swindles millions of dollars from his company. Maybe he even does it in a "legalized" manner, but just the same he's stealing from employees, shareholders, customers . . . and getting away with it. Workers might lose their jobs, pensions, and homes; shareholders might lose their savings; and sometimes innocent bystanders (taxpayers) get stuck with the bill. All because the exec, who got paid the really big bucks, was supposedly "managing" a corporation but secretly lining his own pockets at the expense of everyone else. It's maddening!

That's probably a little how Jesus felt when he was speaking to the religious leaders of his day, because these guys were a lot like that corrupt executive. Except that their job was to manage God's business. They were supposed to be caring for the spiritual needs of their people. Instead they were burying people in crazy religious rules, as well as extracting money and goods—essentially giving God a bad name. No wonder Jesus was so aggravated at them!

The story Jesus tells about the landowner and the vineyard is really about the religious leaders and how they've taken advantage of God's generosity, how they've mismanaged his people, and how they'll eventually kill God's Son. It's not a happy story, but it's one that needs to be told. And the message we can take away is that God gives everyone something of value to manage, and when we handle it his way, our story will have a happy ending.

My Prayer

Dear God,
Thank you for entrusting me with things like life, talents, family, and friends. Please help me to take good care of all you have given me. Amen.

Final Word

> Be strong in the Lord and in his mighty power.
>
> Ephesians 6:10 NIV

Stone
for the Journey

With God's help, I can manage what he puts in my life.

11

Love Driven

> *Whoever has my commands and obeys them, he is the one who loves me. He who loves me will be loved by my Father, and I too will love him and show myself to him.*
>
> John 14:21 NIV

Love is a mysterious thing, and there are many different kinds of love. Certainly, you can love a great pair of shoes, but not in the same way you love your mom or dad. You can love your grandmother's lasagna, but hopefully not as much as you love your grandmother. You can love playing soccer, but not as much as you love your best friend. Loving a pet might be intense, but it's not anything like how you'll feel when you fall in love.

Love is one of those complicated words with a whole lot of different meanings. But there is something that all the various forms of love have in common—motivation to act differently. Loving a great pair of shoes might motivate you to save up your money to purchase them. Loving your grandmother's lasagna might motivate you to pop on over to her house for Sunday dinner. Loving your best friend might motivate you to go out of your way to make him or her happy. Because you love someone or something, you're not concerned about the effort it takes or what it might cost—it's like you don't even think about it. That's because your love is driving you—your love is what motivates you into action.

That's how Jesus wants you to feel about him. He wants you to love him so much that you're motivated to do what he asks you to. He's the reason you obey his commands—why you can love others. This is because he loves you! He will ask you to do only the things that are good for you. Even if something feels hard, it will get easier if love motivates you—and in the end, it will be for your best.

My Prayer

Dear God,
Thank you for loving me! Please help my love for you to grow, and let that love motivate me to do what you ask me to.
Amen.

Stone
for the Journey

Because I love Jesus, I will obey him.

Final Word

> *This I pray, that your love may abound still more and more in real knowledge and all discernment, so that you may approve the things that are excellent, in order to be sincere and blameless until the day of Christ.*
>
> Philippians 1:9–10 NASB

The Cornerstone

The stone the masons threw out is now the cornerstone. This is God's work; we rub our eyes, we can hardly believe it! This is the way it is with you. God's kingdom will be taken back from you and handed over to a people who will live out a kingdom life. Whoever stumbles on this Stone gets shattered; whoever the Stone falls on gets smashed.

Matthew 21:42–44 Message

If you look at the Empire State Building, you will see more than 1,450 feet of astounding height. A truly stunning building, it towers over New York City with an art deco style and a metropolitan majesty that is impossible to miss. But what is it that you don't see? Most people probably never think about the fifty-five-foot foundation that lurks underneath this amazing building. They can't even see it, but even if they could, it's not much to look at—just an enormous solid mass buried beneath the ground. Yet it's this very foundation that anchors that huge building to the earth. Unseen but essential.

As important as that foundation is, it's the cornerstone that really holds things together. The cornerstone, an integral part of the foundation, is the piece that ensures the building is straight and level and square. Without a true cornerstone, the Empire State Building would tip, the structure would fall, and all that would be left is a heap of rubble.

Jesus is like that cornerstone. He is the true foundational piece that God built his church on. Yet the religious leaders of Jesus's day rejected him and his truth. Is it any wonder that their world fell apart after they tossed him aside?

Jesus wants to be your cornerstone as well. He wants to be that solid rock, straight and true, that you build your life on. When you are securely anchored to him, you will be strong enough to withstand the worst earthquake.

My Prayer

Dear God,
Thank you for being my rock-solid cornerstone. Help me to build my life on your foundation. Amen.

Stone
for the Journey

Jesus is foundational to my life.

Final Word

Come to Jesus Christ. He is the living stone that people have rejected, but which God has chosen and highly honored.

1 Peter 2:4 CEV

13

Teachable

If people love me, they will obey my teaching. My Father will love them, and we will come to them and make our home with them. Those who do not love me do not obey my teaching. This teaching that you hear is not really mine; it is from my Father, who sent me.

John 14:23–24 NCV

*Y*ou've probably heard of the school of hard knocks (SHK). Maybe you've heard that it's the people with the hardest heads that attend that school. Some SHK students eventually figure things out, graduate, and move on. But some just keep repeating first grade over and over again. Why do you think some people insist on learning things the hard way? Is it because they're stubborn and thickheaded, and that's the only way to get through to them?

It could be they're slow learners or resistant to learning something new. Or maybe they're snoozing in class or drawing cartoons when they should be listening. Whatever their reasons, some people set themselves up to be unteachable. They think they already know it all, and no one can teach them anything. Unfortunately, that's the kind of attitude that sets a person up to be stupid.

Jesus wants you to embrace learning and to be teachable. He longs for you to love him so much, to trust him so completely, that you're eager to learn from him. He wants you to train your ears to recognize his quiet voice—the one that comes from his Spirit inside of you—so you can know when he's directing you and you can avoid learning things the hard way. Sometimes that quiet voice will tell you to wait on something because Jesus knows the timing isn't right. Sometimes that voice will tell you to speak up about something because Jesus knows the timing is perfect. But if you're not teachable, if you don't listen, you will miss out.

How teachable are you?

My Prayer

Dear God,
I want to be teachable. I want you to live in me and direct me, and I want to be quick to listen and learn. Please help me do that.
Amen.

Stone
for the Journey

When I am teachable, I can learn.

Final Word

Whatever you have learned or received or heard from me, or seen in me—put it into practice. And the God of peace will be with you.

Philippians 4:9 NIV

Prihorities

Priorities

Words from the Rock

"Let me see one of the coins used for paying taxes."
They brought him a silver coin, and he asked,
"Whose picture and name are on it?"
"The Emperor's," they answered.
Then Jesus told them, "Give the Emperor what
belongs to him and give God what belongs to
God."

Matthew 22:19–21 CEV

The religious leaders are at it again. Hoping to trap Jesus in a tricky question about taxes, which has always been a controversial subject, they ask him whether it's fair to pay taxes or not. In those days, taxation was more corrupt than ever. Most of the tax collectors were a slippery bunch of private contractors who went around demanding taxes from their own countrymen in a random and unfair way—adjusting the rates to whatever suited them at the moment. Then they would pocket much of what they collected and give the Roman government the rest. In most people's eyes, tax collectors were no better than thieves, and maybe even worse.

The religious leaders figure that if Jesus says it's fine to tax, it might seem he's condoning thievery. If he says it's wrong to tax, it's like suggesting they can break the law. Either answer can land Jesus in hot water. Or so the religious leaders hope. But instead of falling into their trap, Jesus asks them to show him a Roman coin (the kind used to pay taxes) and then asks them whose picture is on the coin. Of course, they say it's the emperor's image.

That's when Jesus turns the tables. He takes what they'd meant for trickery and uses it to make a crucial statement. He tells them to give the emperor what belongs to him and to give God what belongs to him. Jesus's answer shocks them so much that they just shake their heads and walk away.

What a point Jesus has made—it's as if he said, "Hey, taxes are just money, here today and gone tomorrow. But your soul was created by God, and it's meant to last for all eternity. Which is more important?" As usual, Jesus cuts through the crud and brings the topic back to what really matters. Who do you serve—God or man?

My Prayer

Dear God,
Thank you for reminding me of what matters most. Help me to keep my priorities in order and always put you at the top of my list. Amen.

Stone
for the Journey

God gave me my life. I give it back.

Final Word

We are like clay jars in which this treasure is stored. The real power comes from God and not from us.

2 Corinthians 4:7 CEV

Gentle Reminders

Words from the Rock

> *These things I have spoken to you while abiding with you. But the Helper, the Holy Spirit, whom the Father will send in My name, He will teach you all things, and bring to your remembrance all that I said to you.*
>
> John 14:25–26 NASB

*S*ome people use Post-it notes to remind themselves of things to do, errands to run, or someone to call. But sometimes Post-its are small and get overlooked. Or if you have too many, they become a sea of bright-colored squares with no meaning. Also, they can lose their stickiness and fall off and get lost. So they might not be the most reliable reminders. And sometimes you need a good reminder.

Let's say you have to get up early in the morning to take the SAT test. Maybe you set your alarm clock or rely on your computer's alarm to wake you . . . but what if there's a power outage? So you set your cell phone to go off, but what if the battery runs down? Finally, it might occur to you that the safest plan would be to have a person wake you up—like dear old Mom or Dad. They probably paid for the SAT test, so they wouldn't let you down.

Jesus knew that you'd need spiritual reminders too. That's just one more reason he decided to send his Spirit to live inside of you. Better than an alarm clock or a cell phone or even your parents, God's Spirit can nudge you when you need it. He can quietly warn you to take a different route, or jog your memory about a promise you made to God, or remind you of how much Jesus loves you, or teach you something completely new. The question is, are you tuned in and listening?

My Prayer

Dear God,
Thank you for sending your Spirit to keep me on track and teach me new things about you. Help me to tune in so I can hear the direction you give me.
Amen.

Stone
for the Journey

Through his Spirit, God reminds me of his love.

Final Word

Letting your sinful nature control your mind leads to death. But letting the Spirit control your mind leads to life and peace.

Romans 8:6 NLT

16

Priceless Peace

I am leaving you with a gift—peace of mind and heart. And the peace I give is a gift the world cannot give. So don't be troubled or afraid.

John 14:27 NLT

*S*ome people spend their whole lives looking for something they cannot see, touch, hear, smell, or taste. Yet they long for this intangible thing like a starving man longs for food. Some people spend fortunes and purchase expensive homes, cars, boats—material possessions that they dream will deliver this elusive entity—and even when their money is gone, they remain unsatisfied. Some travel the globe, climb mountains, sit at the feet of gurus, and even withdraw in solitude in pursuit of this hard-to-find thing. A few go so far as to practice forms of self-torture and deprivation in the hopes that they will secure this obscure thing, yet it evades them. They cannot get their hands on it.

What is it they so diligently seek? What is it their souls crave? *Peace.* Peace of mind and peace of heart—a deep inner peace that the world doesn't offer, a peace that cannot be earned or bought. Jesus says that kind of peace is a priceless gift that only he can give. And he gives it to you for free. A priceless gift . . . *for free.*

In an era when prescription drugs, sleeping aids, and other pseudo substitutes for peace are more popular than ever, Jesus's peace is unique—one of a kind. It's the kind of inner calm that can keep you from losing it when everything around you is falling apart—a peace and assurance that can exist in the midst of chaos. Why wouldn't everyone be lining up to receive this kind of peace from Jesus? Why would you look anywhere else for it?

If people understood the depth and power of this peace, they wouldn't settle for anything less. Would you?

My Prayer

Dear God,
Thank you that your peace is a free gift. Remind me to come to you daily to receive this gift. Show me how to share this peace with others. Amen.

Stone
for the Journey

Jesus's peace can keep me from falling apart.

Final Word

Therefore, since we have been made right in God's sight by faith, we have peace with God because of what Jesus Christ our Lord has done for us.

Romans 5:1 NLT

Simple Laws

> *"Love the Lord your God with all your heart and with all your soul and with all your mind." This is the first and greatest commandment. And the second is like it: "Love your neighbor as yourself."*
>
> Matthew 22:37–39 NIV

The law was a big deal when Jesus walked the earth. Pages upon pages were written, and books were created—all to contain the thousands of religious laws that the leaders concocted on a regular basis. There were laws for everything imaginable. For instance, on the Sabbath (the day when no one was supposed to work) there were laws for how much you could salvage if your home was on fire. Never mind that you'd have to make dozens of trips since you were allowed to carry only one tiny handful at a time, but if you "broke the law," you'd be penalized later. Sure, your house might have burned to the ground, but you'd still have to relinquish something of value to the priests.

The purpose of these exhaustive and meticulous laws was to keep God's people in line—or so the scribes and legal minds of the day claimed. Then Jesus came along, and just like that, he condensed and streamlined those bulky, ridiculous laws into two straightforward and simple rules. He said to love God with all you have and to love your neighbor as you love yourself. Ironically, if you follow these two rules, you will automatically fulfill the original law (the Ten Commandments that God gave Moses thousands of years ago).

But as it turns out, these two rules, while simple, aren't exactly easy. Jesus understood that. He knew that you'd need his help to love God with every fiber of your being. He knew you'd have to go to him in order to learn how to love other people the way you love yourself. That's how he wanted it to be. He simplified the law so you'd be able to grasp it, but at the same time, he made it so all-encompassing that you'd need him to help you with it every single day of your life.

My Prayer

Dear God,
I choose to love you with all my heart, soul, and mind, and I choose to love others as I love myself. I need your help to keep this commitment. Thank you.
Amen.

Stone
for the Journey

Jesus shows me how to love God and others.

Final Word

This is love for God: to obey his commands. And his commands are not burdensome.

1 John 5:3 NIV

18

Love's Example

You heard me say, "I am going away and I am coming back to you." If you loved me, you would be glad that I am going to the Father, for the Father is greater than I. I have told you now before it happens, so that when it does happen you will believe. I will not speak with you much longer, for the prince of this world is coming. He has no hold on me, but the world must learn that I love the Father and that I do exactly what my Father has commanded me.

John 14:28–31 NIV

*W*hen Jesus tells us, "Love the Lord your God with all your heart and with all your soul and with all your mind," he is not trying to wax poetic. These words are a living by-product of his life. They are straight from his heart. Loving and obeying God is how Jesus lived on earth and why he died. His number one goal and purpose on earth was to be one with the Father and do his Father's will. Jesus proved that he loved his Father with his entire being—heart and soul and mind—by the way he obeyed God. Jesus gave everything; he held back nothing.

So when Jesus tells his disciples that he is going to the Father, he wants them to be happy for him. He wants them to understand how much he loves his Father and how nothing could be better than joining him. But it's not for his own sake that he wants his disciples to grasp this concept. It's because this kind of love is exactly what he hopes *all* his followers will one day experience. Jesus's desire is that we'll love his Father as much as he does. He wants us to follow his example.

Jesus knows that the more you love God, the more you will do what he wants you to. The more you do what God wants you to, the happier you will be. Love motivates you to live differently, and Jesus wants that motivation to draw you closer to his Father. Jesus knows that being one with his Father will satisfy you like nothing else can.

My Prayer

Dear God,
Teach me to love you the way Jesus loves you.
Show me ways I can spend time with you and
honor you. Make me more like Jesus.
Amen.

Stone
for the Journey

My love for God changes who I am.

Final Word

God showed his love for us when he sent his only Son into the world to give us life.

1 John 4:9 CEV

The Hypocrite Trap

Words from the Rock

> *The teachers of the law and the Pharisees . . . make strict rules and try to force people to obey them, but they are unwilling to help those who struggle under the weight of their rules.*
>
> *They do good things so that other people will see them. They . . . love to have the most important seats at feasts and in the synagogues. They love people to greet them with respect in the marketplaces, and they love to have people call them "Teacher."*
>
> Matthew 23:2, 4–7 NCV

*I*s it a coincidence that so many Scriptures containing Jesus's words are directed toward the religious community? Do you think Jesus's warnings about religion apply only to the leaders of his day? Or is there something we can all learn from Jesus's confrontations with religious hypocrites? As unfortunate as it is, sometimes the Christian community experiences some of the same problems as the scribes and Pharisees. Perhaps Jesus wants to remind all of us to beware of the hypocrite trap.

How do you feel about Christians who judge and criticize people with different beliefs? How do you react to Christians who seem to think they're better than nonbelievers? What do you think about Christians who act like they belong to an exclusive club—like their church is for members only? More importantly, what does Jesus think? Is it possible that Jesus regards some Christians as no different from the religious leaders of his day?

Jesus speaks out against those who make rules for the purpose of hurting and excluding others. He takes a stand against those who appear good on the outside but who are selfish and corrupt underneath. He has no patience with those who, under the guise of religion, elevate themselves above everyone else.

Now imagine how Jesus must feel when someone wearing the label of "Christian" does any of those things. How would he react to people who claim to know him but act just like the religious leaders that he took to task on a regular basis? Jesus wants you to guard your heart against religious superiority and hypocrisy. He wants you to love and serve and practice humility—in other words, to imitate him.

My Prayer

Dear God,
Please help me to be on the alert for hypocrisy in my life. Teach me to practice inclusive love. Make me more like you.
Amen.

Stone
for the Journey

Jesus can keep me authentic and free from hypocrisy.

Final Word

When you pray, do not be like the hypocrites, for they love to pray standing in the synagogues and on the street corners to be seen by men. I tell you the truth, they have received their reward in full.

Matthew 6:5 NIV

20

Good Hurts

*I am the Real Vine and my Father is the Farmer.
He cuts off every branch of me that doesn't bear
grapes. And every branch that is grape-bearing
he prunes back so it will bear even more. You
are already pruned back by the message I have
spoken.*

John 15:1–3 Message

*U*nless you live in a vineyard or near an agricultural community, some of Jesus's stories about farming might be lost
on you. But back when Jesus told these stories, most of his listeners
got the meaning—at least on a surface level. It might have taken a
while for the real spiritual message to sink in.

To understand the metaphor that Jesus is using, you need to know
a little about growing grapes and pruning. First of all, for the grapevine to flourish, the dead branches need to be cut off. And when
a branch is healthy, it will produce big clumps of grapes, but the

weight of the grapes can stress, weaken, or even break the branch. A good farmer knows this, and during the dormant season when grapes aren't growing, he'll cut back (prune) the healthy branches so they're not long, stringy, and weak. After they're cut back, they'll be sturdier and more capable of supporting heavy grapes.

Imagine you're a branch connected to the vine (Jesus), and suddenly the farmer (God) is taking a knife to you. After you recover from the fright, you should realize that (1) you're not a dead branch, so he's not permanently removing you, and (2) if he's pruning you back, it's for your own good so you can be stronger and healthier. Even if it hurts for a while, you need to remember that it would hurt a lot more if he didn't prune you and the weight of the grapes just broke you off.

Sometimes life is like that too. You experience something painful, something you can't even figure out, but later on you realize that was the very thing that made you strong.

My Prayer

Dear God,
Help me to remember that sometimes my injuries will make me grow. Sometimes the pain is to make me stronger and more capable to handle life's challenges.
Amen.

Stone
for the Journey

My wounds draw me closer to Jesus.

Final Word

Consider it pure joy, my brothers, whenever you face trials of many kinds, because you know that the testing of your faith develops perseverance.

James 1:2–3 NIV

Spiritual Family

Words from the Rock

All of you are equal as brothers and sisters. . . .
Only God in heaven is your spiritual Father. . . .
You have only one teacher, the Messiah. The great-
est among you must be a servant. But those who
exalt themselves will be humbled, and those who
humble themselves will be exalted.

Matthew 23:8–12 NLT

*J*esus evens the playing field when he says believers are all equals—brothers and sisters. Upon first hearing, it sounds good and sweet, and you can almost hear the birds singing in the trees. But then when you think about it more, you realize that brothers and sisters can start up some rather feisty family feuds. Jesus knew that from personal experience—he had some half brothers. So maybe that's why he adds a bit more to this equalizing concept, pushing us beyond a family of squabbling siblings.

Jesus also points out that his followers must become like servants. What does that mean? And how do you do it? First of all, lose the notion that a servant is an uneducated, dull, unmotivated person—some poor loser who just goes around mopping the floors and saying, "Yes, sir." In Jesus's day, a good servant was smart, trustworthy, thoughtful, skillful, loyal, clever, and a real asset to his employer. In other words, he was a lot like a very devoted friend. In fact, a really good servant might be the best friend an employer ever had—maybe even closer than a sibling.

Jesus gave the example of being a servant like that. He always put the needs of others above his own. And he did practical things like healing the sick and feeding the hungry.

Now Jesus takes his teaching one step further by saying that when you refuse to be a servant and when you decide to put yourself above others, you will be knocked down and humiliated. Maybe not in this life, but eventually. On the other hand, if you put others above yourself and if you strive to be a good servant, you will eventually be lifted up and honored.

My Prayer

Dear God,
Thank you for making your followers equals. Please teach me to be a good servant—smart and loyal and thoughtful. Let me follow your example.
Amen.

Stone
for the Journey

Jesus can teach me to serve others.

Final Word

Love each other as brothers and sisters and honor others more than you do yourself.

Romans 12:10 CEV

Fruit Connection

Remain in me, and I will remain in you. A branch cannot produce fruit alone but must remain in the vine. In the same way, you cannot produce fruit alone but must remain in me.

John 15:4 NCV

Jesus wants his connection and relationship with you to be vital and life giving. You need to cling to Jesus like a healthy branch would cling to the main trunk of a plant—like you are one with it. What's the benefit of this connection? First of all, like a branch growing out of a tree, which receives the nutrients and water that come through the roots and the trunk, you will receive what you need from Jesus to grow and be healthy. That tight connection guarantees that his life (love, forgiveness, teaching) will flow into you. And Jesus's life keeps you vital and hardy and makes you grow. The result of growing healthy and strong is that you'll eventually bear fruit when the season is right.

Keep in mind that the quality of the fruit is dependent on the vitality of the branch. A wimpy, sickly branch can only produce wimpy, sickly fruit, but a healthy branch will yield top-notch fruit.

Now all this talk about fruit is fine if you're a farmer or you're planning to concoct a fruit salad. But what does it mean to you personally? Why do you need fruit in your life?

Fruit is a metaphor for good things. Who doesn't want more good things in their life? Maybe you'd like to be happier—what if you had more joy? Or maybe you'd like more friends—what if you became more patient and kind? Perhaps you'd like to avoid fighting with your parents or a sibling—what if you had more self-control? Those characteristics, and more, are considered the fruit of the Spirit. They are the results of hanging tight with Jesus. Fortunately, these kinds of fruits are more substantial than grapes or apples—with a much longer shelf life too. So stay connected to Jesus, and when the season is right, you'll be surprised and pleased to see what starts cropping up in your life. And so will the people around you.

My Prayer

Dear God,
Please help me to stay tightly connected to Jesus so that his fruit will become a normal part of my life.
Amen.

Stone
for the Journey

My relationship with Jesus brings good things into my life.

Final Word

The fruit of the Spirit is love, joy, peace, patience, kindness, goodness, faithfulness, gentleness and self-control.

Galatians 5:22–23 NIV

23

False Religion's Reward

Words from the Rock

You Pharisees and teachers are in for trouble! You're nothing but show-offs. You're like tombs that have been whitewashed. On the outside they are beautiful, but inside they are full of bones and filth. That's what you are like. Outside you look good, but inside you are evil and only pretend to be good.

Matthew 23:27–28 CEV

You're already aware that Jesus is fed up with the religious leaders of his day. Now, knowing that his earthly hours are limited, he really lays into them in this portion of Scripture. In fact, the twenty-third chapter of Matthew has *thirty-six* verses of scathing condemnation where Jesus holds nothing back. He lays it all out for everyone to see, describing their shameful behavior in great detail and identifying them as liars, cheats, show-offs, hypocrites, tricksters, filth, snakes, and murderers. Finally, he warns them that they're headed for serious trouble. You have to believe that when Jesus, the

Son of God who knows the ins and outs of the entire universe, says someone's in serious trouble, it's going to be bad.

Besides being arrogant, pompous, misleading, self-centered jerks, the religious leaders make themselves even more despicable to Jesus because of their constant attempts to appear good. He describes them as lovely white boxes that are probably ornately carved and attractive to look at—but inside the boxes are the rotting, stinking, putrid remains of cadavers. Not a pretty picture. As disgusting as that image is, it's how Jesus views religious hypocrisy. He cannot stand it.

Jesus wants you to be authentic—willing to admit to your failures and shortcomings. He wants you to live a transparent life in front of your family and friends, not put on false fronts or try to cover up your mistakes. It's through your honesty—and your willingness to have Jesus change you—that others are impacted. When others realize that you're the real deal and that you give God the credit for any goodness in your life, they want to know more.

My Prayer

Dear God,
Please help me to never try to appear better than I am. Keep me away from false religion and hypocrisy. Let me be the real deal so you can shine in me.
Amen.

Stone
for the Journey

My transparency allows Jesus's light to shine.

Final Word

Do everything without complaining or arguing, so that you may become blameless and pure, children of God without fault in a crooked and depraved generation, in which you shine like stars in the universe.

Philippians 2:14–15 NIV

24

Hang Tight

Words from the Rock

I am the vine, you are the branches; he who abides in Me and I in him, he bears much fruit, for apart from Me you can do nothing. If anyone does not abide in Me, he is thrown away as a branch and dries up; and they gather them, and cast them into the fire and they are burned.

John 15:5–6 NASB

emember the grapevine metaphor? Jesus explained the need to prune branches so they'd be strong enough to support the weight of the grapes. But there's another reason to prune the branches. The act of cutting back a branch causes it to regenerate in a way that connects it even more tightly to the main vine or trunk of the plant. The more secure the branch is to the main trunk, the healthier it will be. The trunk literally gives life to the branch. A bad connection—due to things like lack of pruning, infestation, or even a bad storm—will weaken the branch. That's when a farmer might step in and prune it, use something to deal with the bugs, or bind the branch more tightly to the trunk.

The farmer understands that if the branch breaks away from the trunk and dries up, it's all over. Dead branches aren't good for much more than firewood. However, if there's still a little life left in the branch, the farmer can rescue it by grafting it back onto the trunk (or vine). However, the trunk must be wounded to do this so the sap will flow out and into the branch, revive it, and restore the connection—like how Jesus was wounded on the cross so his life could flow into us.

So while God has the work of being the farmer (mending, pruning, grafting), and Jesus has the work of being the main trunk (getting nutrients and water from the soil to the branches), your job (as a branch) is to hang tight to Jesus. Then you'll grow and be healthy and even bear fruit.

My Prayer

Dear God,
Help me to remember that nothing is more important than for me to hang tight to Jesus. Thank you for all you do to keep me connected. Amen.

Stone
for the Journey

Being connected to Jesus brings life.

Final Word

Who will separate us from the love of Christ? Will tribulation, or distress, or persecution, or famine, or nakedness, or peril, or sword?

Romans 8:35 NASB

Wrong Expectations

Words from the Rock

> *O Jerusalem, Jerusalem, the city that kills the prophets and stones God's messengers! How often I have wanted to gather your children together as a hen protects her chicks beneath her wings, but you wouldn't let me. And now, look, your house is abandoned and desolate. For I tell you this, you will never see me again until you say, "Blessings on the one who comes in the name of the LORD!"*
>
> Matthew 23:37–39 NLT

*C*an you hear the anguish in Jesus's voice as he says these words? He's entering the city of Jerusalem, riding on the back of a baby donkey, yet being heralded as the King! People are shouting praises, waving palm branches, and throwing their coats down on the street for this parade. It's an amazing day—feverish excitement and hope charge the air. Everyone can feel it—something amazing is about to take place. So why is Jesus so disturbed? Why is he so saddened?

Since Jesus is God, he knows everything, and he knows that the same people shouting his praises will soon turn against him. It won't be long until they're yelling, "Crucify him!" The reason their hearts change so quickly has to do with their wrong expectations. These people are hungry for a leader. They've been waiting for a powerful king to deliver them from their oppressors (the Roman government). They're even ready to take up arms and fight for their deliverance—if only Jesus would lead them. But Jesus didn't come to fight an earthly battle; he came to win the greatest spiritual war of the ages. Yet the people didn't get this. They had wrong expectations.

It's easy to have wrong expectations about Jesus. Some people come to him expecting him to solve all their problems, but they're reluctant to do his will. Some think Jesus should give them what they want, but they don't realize that Jesus understands their needs better than they do.

Jesus doesn't want you to bring your agenda to him; he wants you to bring your heart. He doesn't want you to tell him what to do; he wants you to listen.

My Prayer

Dear God,
Thank you for loving me so much that you won't let me run the show. I want your will in my life. Help me to set my wrong expectations aside and trust you.
Amen.

Stone
for the Journey

I will set my expectations aside and wait on God.

Final Word

> Don't get tired of helping others. You will be rewarded when the time is right, if you don't give up.
>
> Galatians 6:9 CEV

26

In Sync

If you remain in me and my words remain in you, you may ask for anything you want, and it will be granted! When you produce much fruit, you are my true disciples. This brings great glory to my Father.

John 15:7–8 NLT

*S*ome people hear Jesus's promise like this: "You may ask for anything you want, and it will be granted!" And they get all excited like they just won the lottery, or like Jesus is their personal Santa Claus. They ask for anything and it's theirs—who wouldn't jump on board? So they start making their wish lists. But they overlook the previous line of the verse: "If you remain in me and my words remain in you." What those people don't realize is that there's a prerequisite.

Jesus has already gone to great lengths for you to understand the magnitude of staying connected to him—nothing is more important than that. Now he's saying you're in him and his words are in you. That's a very intimate connection. It means your mind, heart, and soul are planted firmly in Jesus, and his words are buried deep inside of you. It's not simply being connected to Jesus; it's being completely enmeshed with him until he's such a part of you that you think, live, love, and act like him. It's a position that every believer should aspire to, but it will take a lot of surrendering on your part. If you reach that place of connectedness, you will be able to ask for anything you want and get it—because you will be asking for what Jesus wants too. You and Jesus will be in perfect sync.

But it's a process, and just like the vine must stay attached to the trunk so that in the right season and time it will bear fruit, you too must remain connected to Jesus. When you are one with Jesus, you can ask for anything—and you will get it.

My Prayer

Dear God,
Please help me to remain in you, and let your words and your will remain in me so that together we can do amazing things!
Amen.

Final Word

If you're serious about living this new resurrection life with Christ, act like it. Pursue the things over which Christ presides.

Colossians 3:1 Message

Stone
for the Journey

When I am in sync with Jesus, I can ask for anything and he will do it.

27

Impressions

> *Jesus then left the Temple. As he walked away,*
> *his disciples pointed out how very impressive the*
> *Temple architecture was. Jesus said, "You're not*
> *impressed by all this sheer size, are you? The truth*
> *of the matter is that there's not a stone in that*
> *building that is not going to end up in a pile of*
> *rubble."*
>
> Matthew 24:1–2 Message

*W*hen Jesus's disciples see the temple in Jerusalem, they comment on its immense size and amazing stature. It was an incredible structure, unlike anything on earth at that time. Who wouldn't have been impressed?

Jesus.

Think about it. Jesus is God's Son. God created the earth and the entire universe. God designed heaven (which is unimaginable to the human mind). Jesus is part of God, and because they are one, Jesus participated in all those locations and events and creations. Jesus had seen it all. It would be kind of like if you'd grown up in Disney World—you'd not only ridden all the rides, but you also helped to design them. Then you visit another town, and the kids there act like their little Podunk amusement park is the greatest thing ever. You probably wouldn't be too impressed.

What would it take to impress Jesus? Not buildings or roads or bridges or stones piled on each other. Those things can't compare to what Jesus knows exists in the greater universe. What impresses him is when you believe him, obey him, trust him, and love him with your whole heart, soul, and mind. That's the only thing you can do to make an impression on Jesus—when you make your life an impression of his.

My Prayer

Dear God,
I know sometimes I am impressed by the wrong things. Help me to remember what's really important and to live a life that impresses you.
Amen.

> **Stone**
> *for the Journey*
>
> **Jesus's impression on me is impressive.**

Final Word

I realize how kind God has been to me, and so I tell each of you not to think you are better than you really are. Use good sense and measure yourself by the amount of faith that God has given you.

Romans 12:3 CEV

Stay in Love

28

Words from the Rock

As the Father has loved me, so have I loved you.
Now remain in my love.

John 15:9 NIV

Human beings have some basic needs, including air, food, water . . . and love. It's true, love is as necessary as the air we breathe. As sad as it is, there's actual medical testimony about orphaned infants who've declined physically and even died for lack of love from their caregivers. Love is essential to life. But not only human love. We are created with a natural longing for another kind of love too. Our souls are designed to crave a deeper sort of love—a life-giving, spiritual love that comes only from God.

Jesus is the conduit of that love. God's love pours through Jesus to us. The only condition is that we stay linked to Jesus. He asks us to remain in his love. The word *remain* means "to stay put," "to linger," "to wait," "to hang about," "to stick around." It's something we automatically want to do when we love someone—we want to be with them.

What if someone gave you the latest, greatest video game console and every game and accessory that came with it? You get all set up and ready to play when you realize there's no power cord, so you have absolutely no way to connect this console to electricity. No other power cord will work, and consequently, the console won't work and you can't play a single game. Talk about frustration.

That missing power cord is kind of like Jesus. Without him, there's no connection to God. God's love (like power to the console) is transmitted when you are plugged into Jesus—when you remain in his love. So how's your connection? Are you plugged in?

My Prayer

Dear God,
I want to stay linked to Jesus so that your love will pour through him into me. Please show me everyday ways to keep myself plugged in.
Amen.

Stone
for the Journey

**Jesus is the
conduit of
God's love
to me.**

Final Word

If we believe that Jesus is truly Christ, we are God's children. Everyone who loves the Father will also love his children.

1 John 5:1 CEV

What's Next?

29

Words from the Rock

See to it that no one misleads you. For many will come in My name, saying, "I am the Christ," and will mislead many. You will be hearing of wars and rumors of wars. See that you are not frightened, for those things must take place, but that is not yet the end. For nation will rise against nation, and kingdom against kingdom, and in various places there will be famines and earthquakes. But all these things are merely the beginning of birth pangs.

Matthew 24:4–8 NASB

For more than two thousand years, generations after generations of believers have been expecting and predicting the end of the world. Many of them expected it to end within their own generation—for good reason too. The atrocities that happened during some people's lifetimes were enough to make anyone long for life as they knew it to come to a screeching halt. Religious persecution, torturous deaths, bloody religious wars, plagues and pestilences, droughts and floods, earthquakes and hurricanes . . . all seemed to indicate that the end of the earth was near.

So predictions continued, and sometimes churches created doctrines based on their predictions. Sometimes they picked dates for when the earth would end. Some still pick dates today.

What is Jesus's response to all this? He says that all these things will happen—wars, famines, earthquakes—and that they're just "the beginning of birth pangs." What does that mean? The moment of childbirth is unpredictable. Some women experience only a few birth pains and then give birth. Some experience hours and even days of birth pains—which feel like an eternity—and finally the baby is born. In other words, it could be a short time or a long time. Only God knows.

Guess what? The end *is* near. In fact, it will be within your lifetime. Yet you don't even know how long your lifetime will be, so how can you know the end is near? Because everyone's earthly life will end. It always does. So whether your end will be a death of natural means or a result of the predicted "end of the world" is kind of irrelevant. It will happen. The question is, will you be ready?

My Prayer

Dear God,
Only you know when the end of the earth will be. Please help me to focus on staying connected to you instead of worrying about things I cannot control.
Amen.

Stone
for the Journey

Jesus holds my future in his hands.

Final Word

This one who is life itself was revealed to us, and we have seen him. And now we testify and proclaim to you that he is the one who is eternal life. He was with the Father, and then he was revealed to us.

1 John 1:2 NLT

30

Real Joy

Words from the Rock

*If you keep My commandments, you will abide
in My love; just as I have kept My Father's commandments and abide in His love. These things I
have spoken to you so that My joy may be in you,
and that your joy may be made full.*

John 15:10–11 NASB

Joy—real joy—can be almost as elusive as peace. It is one
of those things people constantly seek out but is extremely
hard to find. Sometimes people think they've found it when they
experience a rush or a thrill or a pleasant surprise. The problem is
that kind of joy doesn't usually stick around for long. Now you see
it, now you don't. Unfortunately, that small jolt of joy can sometimes
set people up to attempt to find it again.

Most of the time, joy seekers look in all the wrong places. They
might try extreme adventures, alcohol abuse, sexual experimentation,
illegal drugs, or other dangerous activities in the hopes of finding a

real thrill. But even when they experience a counterfeit sort of joy, it never lasts. Consequently, they might get trapped into an addictive behavior—chasing after that elusive rush they imagine exists.

The joy that Jesus offers is real and lasting. This joy comes as the result of participating in a committed, loving relationship with him. When you love Jesus so much that you're willing to live your life the way he wants you to, you will experience a fulfilling sense of joy. Sure, it might not be a giddy, crazy, roller-coaster sort of joy, but it will be authentic. It will be a joy that you can feel deep inside of you—a joy that will stay with you, bolstering your spirit during hard times. As your commitment to God grows stronger, it will be a joy that others will notice when they look at you.

Don't be tricked into seeking a counterfeit joy. Go to God for the real deal.

My Prayer

Dear God,
Please help me not to fall into the trap of looking for earthly joy. Remind me that when I love and obey you, your joy will become part of my life.
Amen.

Stone
for the Journey

God's joy comes when I obey him out of love.

Final Word

Do not throw away your confidence; it will be richly rewarded.

Hebrews 10:35 NIV

Grim Warnings

Words from the Rock

They are going to throw you to the wolves and kill you, everyone hating you because you carry my name. And then, going from bad to worse, it will be dog-eat-dog, everyone at each other's throat, everyone hating each other.

In the confusion, lying preachers will come forward and deceive a lot of people. For many others, the overwhelming spread of evil will do them in—nothing left of their love but a mound of ashes.

Matthew 24:9–12 Message

Jesus spoke some frightening words to his disciples here. As sensational and grim as this forecast sounded, all that he predicted eventually happened during his disciples' lifetimes. Because Jesus loved them, he wanted them to know the truth and to be forewarned.

There's something comforting about knowing what's around the next corner—even when it's something bad. For instance, an army that's about to be attacked would find it helpful to know some of the enemy's strategies and plans in advance. It would allow them to prepare themselves, plan a better line of defense, and hopefully suffer fewer casualties.

Following Jesus will not always be a walk in the park. It's not supposed to be easy-breezy. Hard times will definitely come your way—in fact, they'll make you grow stronger. If you let him, Jesus will stand by your side through those times; he will help you. Even though you probably won't suffer the same way his disciples did (some were burned, beaten, crucified, boiled in oil . . . and almost all died gruesome deaths), you will experience some suffering and persecution simply because of your relationship with Jesus. When someone does attack you for your faith, you can be thankful—it shows you really do belong to God.

My Prayer

Dear God,
I know that following you is supposed to come with some challenges. Remind me to ask you for help when they come my way.
Amen.

Stone
for the Journey

My relationship with God will bring some opposition.

Final Word

We live by faith, not by sight.
2 Corinthians 5:7 NIV

Sacrificial Love

Words from the Rock

*Now I tell you to love each other, as I have loved
you. The greatest way to show love for friends is
to die for them.*

John 15:12–13 CEV

*D*o you think you'd jump in front of a freight train to save
your best friend's life if it meant you got killed in the
process? Tough question, isn't it? You probably wish you could say
yes, of course—you love your friend so much you'd willingly relinquish your life for him or her. But what would actually happen
when the rubber met the road (or the steel wheels met the tracks)?
Would you really give up your last breath for someone else? The
truth is you might not be as brave or selfless as you'd like to think.
Not many people are.

When Jesus told his friends this, he knew that he would soon be
giving up everything, including his earthly life, for them. The reason
he could make this sacrifice—and make it willingly—was because

he loved them so much. Jesus knew that by surrendering his life, he was securing eternity for all who believed in him. His death was the greatest expression of his love. And he tells us to love each other with that same kind of commitment and intensity. But what does it mean? Seriously, how often does a person have to leap in front of a train to rescue a friend?

While it's somewhat unlikely that you'll physically give up your life for a friend, there are other ways to imitate Jesus's example of love. Every time you put someone else's interests above your own, set aside your own selfishness for them, or inconvenience yourself to help them, you are in essence dying to yourself. When you make personal sacrifices for the benefit of others, you practice the kind of selfless love that Jesus described.

My Prayer

Dear God,
Help me to put other people's needs above my own. Please remind me when I'm being selfish, and show me how to grow up in the way I love others.
Amen.

Stone
for the Journey

With God's help, I can love others selflessly.

Final Word

Anyone who claims to live in God's light and hates a brother or sister is still in the dark. It's the person who loves brother and sister who dwells in God's light and doesn't block the light from others.

1 John 2:9–10 Message

33

Everyone's Chance

Words from the Rock

Because of the increase of wickedness, the love of most will grow cold, but he who stands firm to the end will be saved. And this gospel of the kingdom will be preached in the whole world as a testimony to all nations, and then the end will come.

Matthew 24:12–14 NIV

*A*gain Jesus is talking about what some people call the "last days." Remember, no matter what era believers live in (whether it's AD 12 or 2012), everyone experiences their own "last day." Everyone's earthly life will eventually end—it's inevitable. Yet here Jesus is warning that during your lifetime there might come some really hard challenges (like the death of a loved one, a broken heart, or a major disappointment). There might be times when it feels like your love for Jesus cools off, but he promises that if you hold on—if your faith doesn't crumble—you will be safe in the end.

Then Jesus gives us a clue as to when the end of the world actually will come. He says that after every single person on the planet has heard about him, including people from the most remote regions of upper Mongolia or sub-Saharan Africa or the Amazon rain forest—when they hear about Jesus's love for them and that he offers them forgiveness and a relationship with him—that's when the world as we know it will come to an end. That's when a new world will begin.

How will you participate in this monumental plan? What can you do right there in your own part of the world to help others come to know Jesus? How can you show his love and mercy to someone in your life? When you do this—when you share the gospel message by living the kind of life God wants you to—you help to change history!

My Prayer

Dear God,
I want you to use me to show others your love and grace. Live through me so they can see you. Amen.

Final Word

Jesus lived the truth of this commandment, and you also are living it. For the darkness is dis-appearing, and the true light is already shining.

1 John 2:8 NLT

Stone
for the Journey

God can use me to send a message of love to others.

34

True Friends

Words from the Rock

*You are My friends if you do what I command you.
No longer do I call you slaves, for the slave does not
know what his master is doing; but I have called
you friends, for all things that I have heard from
My Father I have made known to you.*

John 15:14–15 NASB

*D*o you realize the enormity of being called God's friends?
Before Jesus came to earth to show us God's love, people
felt distanced from God. The idea of being intimate with God, actually being considered his friend, was more far-fetched than expecting
the president of the United States to invite you to dinner with the
first family. It was like there was an insurmountable wall between
people and God.

In fact, there was a huge curtain that hung in the temple where
people gathered to worship God. These multiple layers of draperies
were thick and heavy (like a wall) and were designed to separate God

from his worshipers. This curtain symbolized a division—God on one side and the people on the other. After Jesus died on the cross, this thick curtain was miraculously split open from top to bottom to show that the wall dividing God from man was gone.

Jesus doesn't want anything to come between you and God. He wants to be your closest friend. Think about the kind of relationship that best friends have. Don't they usually tell each other everything? Don't they share secrets and confessions? In the same way, Jesus promises that as your intimate friend, he will tell you everything God has told him. No secrets. Full disclosure. Naturally, he expects you to be open and honest like that with him, because that's what friends do.

My Prayer

Dear God,
Thank you for being my friend. Help me to be a better friend to you and not hold anything back, because I know I can trust you with all my secrets.
Amen.

> **Stone**
> *for the Journey*
>
> **When I'm God's friend, he shows me what I need to know.**

Final Word

You are God's chosen and special people. You are a group of royal priests and a holy nation. God has brought you out of darkness into his marvelous light. Now you must tell all the wonderful things that he has done.

1 Peter 2:9 CEV

35

Troubling Times

Words from the Rock

This is going to be trouble on a scale beyond what the world has ever seen, or will see again. If these days of trouble were left to run their course, nobody would make it. But on account of God's chosen people, the trouble will be cut short.

Matthew 24:21–22 Message

*I*f you've ever run a marathon, you know that the last couple of miles are the worst. Your body is spent, each step feels harder than the last, and your lungs are aching. Some runners feel like they're about to die during the final grueling minutes of a race like that. Some even quit.

What if you're running a marathon and feeling so exhausted that you don't really think you can make the final two miles? You think, *Maybe next year. . . .* Then, out of the blue, the finish line is right in front of you—either your mileage estimation was wrong or someone shortened the distance of the marathon. Whatever the case, you'd be very glad to see that finish line.

In a small way, that's like what Jesus is describing. He's saying that troubles will come and that times will get hard. Remember how he promised to keep us informed because we're his friends? He doesn't trick us into believing that our lives will be all sweet and easy. He makes no secret that some challenges lie ahead. But he also promises that when we belong to him, he will cut the hard times short. In other words, he won't let us go through anything that's too much to bear.

God knows what we're made of and how much we can take. Because he loves us, he won't bury us in trouble—but he does expect us to call on him for help. At the same time, he knows that trying ordeals really do make us stronger—and like a marathon runner, the stronger we get, the longer we can run.

My Prayer

Dear God,
I know that my life isn't supposed to be easy. Remind me to ask you for help and to remember that you don't give me more than I can take.
Amen.

Stone
for the Journey

When I depend on God, he sees me through.

Final Word

Join with me in suffering for the gospel, by the power of God, who has saved us and called us to a holy life—not because of anything we have done but because of his own purpose and grace.

2 Timothy 1:8–9 NIV

36

Chosen

You didn't choose me. I chose you. I appointed you
to go and produce lasting fruit, so that the Father
will give you whatever you ask for, using my name.
This is my command: Love each other.

John 15:16–17 NLT

o you know how it feels to be lined up and waiting to be chosen for a team? Like when team captains take turns picking the best athletes or their best friends to be on their team. Along with everyone else who's waiting, you don't want to be the last one standing there. You don't want to feel humiliated when you see disappointment wash over the face of the team captain who gets stuck with you.

You will never have to experience that kind of uncertainty and insecurity with Jesus. He points directly at you and says, "I want you. You belong with me. I need you on my team. Come on, let's go!" Jesus makes it clear right from the start that he chose you even before you knew him—he picked you to join him on a great adventure. He wants you with him.

Jesus also invites you to participate in his plan—his plan to reach out to others. The way he expects you to do that is actually fairly simple, and it's something that should sound familiar by now. Jesus reminds you of his commandment to love each other—repeating it often because he knows you need to hear it again and again. In the same way he chose you, the same way he made you his friend, the same way he loves you . . . he wants you to choose others, befriend others, and love others. That's how you show you're on Jesus's team.

My Prayer

Dear God,
Thank you for choosing me! Teach me to spot people who need to be included, and help me to reach out to them. Please show me new ways to love others.
Amen.

Stone
for the Journey

God chose me to show his love to others.

Final Word

Love means doing what God has commanded us, and he has commanded us to love one another, just as you heard from the beginning.

2 John 6 NLT

37

Don't Be Tricked

Words from the Rock

If anyone tells you, "There [Jesus] is, out in the desert," do not go out; or, "Here he is, in the inner rooms," do not believe it. For as lightning that comes from the east is visible even in the west, so will be the coming of the Son of Man.

Matthew 24:26–27 NIV

Jesus is well aware that scam artists and charlatans have been around since the beginning of time, and he knows there are more to come. He also understands that many frauds will get involved in religion. So he warns you not to be deceived if someone tells you they can take you to see Jesus. You don't need to join a special group or go to a special place to be with Jesus. Those are the lines of a trickster.

There are several reasons people set up religious scams. Some frauds just want to get rich, and they know how to pick out people vulnerable to scams—people who are spiritually lost and desperate enough to believe they can buy their salvation. Other tricksters are so full of themselves and their false ideals that they hope to gather a following.

Some people have been tricked and don't realize it. Jesus doesn't want you to be deceived. He wants you to beware if someone suggests that giving money or services will secure your spot in heaven. He wants you to be skeptical if someone offers to "take you somewhere" to find Jesus. Don't forget that you have Jesus's Spirit to guide you— and that quiet discernment will help you to suspect when something's not quite right.

Jesus promises that when he comes, you will know it. In the same way you can hear a boom of thunder and see a flash of lightning in the sky, you will know without a doubt when Jesus shows up. It'll be a big deal! Anyone who tries to tell you differently is probably trying to trick you. Don't fall for it.

My Prayer

Dear God,
Teach me how to be wise and not fall for anyone's tricks. I know I can trust you and that you make yourself known in ways that are indisputable.
Amen.

Stone
for the Journey

When my eyes are on Jesus, I cannot be tricked.

Final Word

Things that are seen don't last forever, but things that are not seen are eternal. That's why we keep our minds on the things that cannot be seen.

2 Corinthians 4:18 CEV

38

Citizens of Heaven

Words from the Rock

> *If the people of this world hate you, just remember that they hated me first. If you belonged to the world, its people would love you. But you don't belong to the world. I have chosen you to leave the world behind, and that is why its people hate you.*
>
> John 15:18–19 CEV

When visiting foreign lands, you carry a passport with you. The obvious reason is that most countries won't let you in without one. But it's also a useful source of ID. If you plan to stay for an extended time in a foreign country, you'll need a visa as well. Visas and passports are the way that government officials identify what nation you belong to and where you have your citizenship. It's how the world at large works, and life goes a lot more smoothly when you know the laws of the land.

In some ways, the spiritual world is not that much different. Once you belong to God, your citizenship is in heaven. Sure, you're here on earth for the time being, but Jesus is like your passport—you are identified as his, and it's because of him that your allegiance is with heaven. As a result, you might sometimes be treated like a foreigner in this world, and sometimes foreigners aren't made to feel very welcome. In fact, Jesus says that if people hate him (and some do), they will likewise hate you. So you shouldn't be surprised when they do.

It might be a little easier to accept this kind of negative reaction when you realize that hatred and prejudice are products of ignorance. Some people, like those in other countries or cultures, might automatically dismiss or judge what they don't know or understand. So people who don't know Jesus might dislike him. That's when it's helpful to remember that Jesus wants you to be his ambassador and to love others. Hopefully then they will begin to see Jesus for who he really is—and they might become interested in gaining citizenship in his kingdom too!

My Prayer

Dear God,
Thank you for reminding me that my real home is in heaven with you. Please help me to reach out to others while I'm here on earth.
Amen.

Stone
for the Journey

Jesus is my passport while I live on earth.

Final Word

Now we know that if the earthly tent we live in is destroyed, we have a building from God, an eternal house in heaven, not built by human hands.

2 Corinthians 5:1 NIV

39

Earth's Final Day

Words from the Rock

Then at last, the sign that the Son of Man is coming will appear in the heavens, and there will be deep mourning among all the peoples of the earth. And they will see the Son of Man coming on the clouds of heaven with power and great glory. And he will send out his angels with the mighty blast of a trumpet, and they will gather his chosen ones from all over the world—from the farthest ends of the earth and heaven.

Matthew 24:30–31 NLT

*Y*ou've probably heard that all good things must come to an end. Sometimes that sounds a bit dismal. Say you're celebrating a special birthday and it's been so amazing—the best day ever—and you really, really don't want it to be over. Unfortunately, there's not a thing you can do to stop the day from ending. When midnight comes, that's it. When it's over, it's over. The end.

Maybe it's kind of like that when you think about the earth coming to an end. Maybe the thought of this planet's last day leaves you feeling a little concerned—or even totally freaked out. After all, there are some pretty cool things about the earth—hopefully you appreciate and enjoy them. Maybe you love a particular snowy mountain that's great for snowboarding. Or you might love the ocean, the sound of the waves tumbling in one after the next. Or perhaps there's a particular tree that means a lot to you, or you like the way the grass smells after it's been cut. You can't picture all of that just coming to a screeching halt—end of story.

Can you remember how you felt as a little kid? Maybe you didn't want your childhood to end; you didn't want to grow up. But time passes . . . and suddenly you're old enough to drive and do some other pretty cool things, and you realize you wouldn't go back to being a five-year-old for anything. The ending of one good thing led to the beginning of something far better.

God's plan for the earth to end is so there can be a new beginning. And God's new beginning will be way better than what has just ended—far greater than anything you can imagine!

My Prayer

Dear God,
I'm so glad I can trust you with endings and beginnings. Help me not only to be ready but also to eagerly anticipate whatever you're bringing my way.
Amen.

Stone
for the Journey

When God ends something, he begins something even better.

Final Word

Now it is God who has made us for this very purpose and has given us the Spirit as a deposit, guaranteeing what is to come.

2 Corinthians 5:5 NIV

40

Our Example

Words from the Rock

> *When that happens, remember this: Servants don't get better treatment than their masters. If they beat on me, they will certainly beat on you. If they did what I told them, they will do what you tell them.*

John 15:20 Message

The unknown can be scary. Whether it's an imagined monster that lurked beneath your bed when you were seven, or the first day at a new high school in a new town, something about not knowing what's around the next corner can be a little freaky. Maybe that's why Jesus spent so many of his last days with his disciples preparing them for what was coming. He knew that his friends were going to face challenges unlike anything they ever had before. He wanted them to be informed and ready.

One of the warnings Jesus gave is in regard to how his followers would be treated. It's kind of like having a big brother who tips you off about the bullies who live down the street, cautioning that he got attacked by them and that you should be on your guard too. He's our example. In other words, if someone doesn't like Jesus, they probably won't like you either.

On the other hand, if people respect Jesus, you can expect them to respect you too. His friends are your friends. Jesus has a lot of friends, which means you do too. He knows that when times get tough—and they will—you'll be comforted by having these kinds of friends around you. And by the same token, Jesus wants you to be the kind of friend that others can lean on during their hard times. He wants you to follow his example and to be as loyal and kind and loving to your friends as he has been to you.

My Prayer

Dear God,
Thanks for giving me a heads-up sometimes. Please teach me to be the kind of friend that others can trust to stand by them.
Amen.

> **Stone**
> *for the Journey*
>
> **Jesus shows me how to love others.**

Final Word

This is how we know what love is: Jesus Christ laid down his life for us. And we ought to lay down our lives for our brothers.

1 John 3:16 NIV

41

Be Aware

Words from the Rock

> *Now learn this lesson from the fig tree: As soon as its twigs get tender and its leaves come out, you know that summer is near. Even so, when you see all these things, you know that it is near, right at the door. I tell you the truth, this generation will certainly not pass away until all these things have happened. Heaven and earth will pass away, but my words will never pass away.*
>
> Matthew 24:32–35 NIV

If you look up at the sky and see ominous, dark clouds rolling in, you might suspect that the weather is changing. Perhaps there's a major thunderstorm coming, and if you're outside, you might even want to make a plan to go somewhere to escape the elements. That's just common sense.

God gave us the physical abilities to see and hear and think in order to avoid perils like tornadoes or hurricanes. But he also gave us a spiritual ability to perceive other kinds of dangers. You are designed to listen with spiritual ears and to see with spiritual eyes. Unlike your physical ears and eyes, your spiritual senses can become dull if they're not used. Jesus wants you to keep them sharp and ready. In the same way you can see storm clouds gathering overhead, you can discern when a spiritual situation is risky. Like you might need to be careful around someone who tries to put words in God's mouth, or a "friend" who encourages you to do something you know is wrong.

The way you can keep your spiritual senses in top form is by spending time with Jesus. The more you keep your spiritual eyes on him and the more you tune your spiritual ears to his voice, the less likely you'll be blindsided. Even if it seems you're surrounded by storms and other threats that Jesus says will come your way—even if everything around you appears to be falling apart—you will remain safe when you're close to Jesus. He has promised to be with you and to protect you through anything.

My Prayer

Dear God,
Help me to remain connected to you, and teach me to tune my spiritual senses in to you. Thank you for keeping me safe in times of trouble. Amen.

Stone
for the Journey

God will help me keep my spiritual senses sharp.

Final Word

Letting your sinful nature control your mind leads to death. But letting the Spirit control your mind leads to life and peace.

Romans 8:6 NLT

42

No Excuses

Words from the Rock

They will do all this to you because of me, for they have rejected the One who sent me. They would not be guilty if I had not come and spoken to them. But now they have no excuse for their sin. Anyone who hates me also hates my Father. If I hadn't done such miraculous signs among them that no one else could do, they would not be guilty. But as it is, they have seen everything I did, yet they still hate me and my Father. This fulfills what is written in their Scriptures: "They hated me without cause."

John 15:21–25 NLT

*Y*ou may have heard that ignorance of the law is no excuse to break it. Imagine you're driving down the highway and don't see a speed limit sign anywhere. Maybe it's a remote area, or maybe a strong windstorm blew all the signs down. You're not really sure how fast you should go, so you decide to drive ninety miles per hour.

Before long you see flashing blue lights in your rearview mirror. You pull over and say to the officer, "Sorry, man, I didn't know what the speed limit was right here." Do you think he'll smile and say, "No problem," then close his little book and walk away? Don't count on it. If you're a licensed driver, you should know what the speed limits are on certain kinds of roads in your state. You should know you need to respect those laws even if a speed limit sign isn't around.

That's kind of like what Jesus is saying here. He's been out in the open in his teachings about God. His listeners aren't ignorant about the coming Messiah. They know about the old prophecies, and they're aware that Jesus has fulfilled many of them by doing miracles (healing people, feeding thousands, raising the dead). Jesus has done everything possible to show everyone that he is God's Son, and the news of his power and authority and influence has spread across the land.

Yet there are those who absolutely refuse to believe him. Like children covering their eyes and ears, some stubbornly choose to reject Jesus, deciding to hate him. Despite the fact that Jesus did everything possible to win them over, they won't listen. Don't be like them. Take Jesus's words to heart—knowing who he is becomes your excuse to love him.

My Prayer

Dear God,
Thank you for showing yourself to me so I have no excuse for not following you. Help me to remember all you've done so my faith remains firm.
Amen.

Stone
for the Journey

I have no excuse not to love Jesus.

Final Word

Now there is no condemnation for those who belong to Christ Jesus. And because you belong to him, the power of the life-giving Spirit has freed you from the power of sin that leads to death.

Romans 8:1–2 NLT

43

Distractions

> *When the Son of Man returns, it will be like it was in Noah's day. In those days before the flood, the people were enjoying banquets and parties and weddings right up to the time Noah entered his boat. People didn't realize what was going to happen until the flood came and swept them all away. That is the way it will be when the Son of Man comes.*
>
> Matthew 24:37–39 NLT

Again Jesus is talking about the end of time and how vital it will be for us to remain connected to him and tuned in. Envision being on an elegant cruise ship out in the middle of the sea. It's one of those mega ships with everything anyone could possibly want to do—lots of swimming pools, a water park, rock climbing, wakeboarding, skeet shooting, golf, restaurants, shopping, theaters . . . and the list goes on. It's a floating party.

Then there's an announcement that something is wrong and that passengers should report to the lifeboat areas. Well, the ship seems solid enough, the sky is blue, and the music is still playing, so the fun continues, and most of the passengers just ignore the warning. They think, *What could possibly be wrong?*

Remember the *Titanic*?

Jesus says it will be somewhat like that in the last days. He warns us that many people will be so distracted with having a good time—partying to the max—that they'll be oblivious to what's really going on and the approaching danger. Like the passengers on the *Titanic*, who felt it was impossible for such a humongous ship to sink, they will ignore the warnings. Many will refuse to get into the lifeboats . . . until it's too late. That's why Jesus wants you to keep tuned in to him. He wants your spiritual ears to be listening and your spiritual eyes to be wide open so you'll know what's coming, so you'll be ready and eagerly waiting. Don't be distracted!

My Prayer

Dear God,
I always want to stay tuned in to you. Help me to realize when something in my life is trying to distract me from you. Keep me connected to you.
Amen.

Stone
for the Journey

When my eyes are on God, I can't be distracted.

Final Word

You have faith in God, whose power will protect you until the last day. Then he will save you, just as he has always planned to do.

1 Peter 1:5 CEV

44

Forever Friend

Words from the Rock

When the Friend I plan to send you from the Father comes—the Spirit of Truth issuing from the Father—he will confirm everything about me. You, too, from your side must give your confirming evidence, since you are in this with me from the start.

John 15:26–27 Message

Sometimes life is just plain hard. Like when everything seems to be going wrong and you're not sure how much more you can take. Maybe your family is dysfunctional—having serious problems and just really messed up. Maybe something at school is making you crazy. Or maybe someone has broken your heart. Is there anything that can make you feel better?

How about a friend? What if you had a really good friend to turn to—someone who was a great listener and knew you better than anyone? What if this friend loved you no matter what and cared deeply about you? What if this person was ubersmart and gave excellent advice? Do you think that would help you feel better? Would it help you through a hard time?

Jesus promises you a friend like that in his Spirit—who is actually part of Jesus. God's Spirit is ready to be an amazing friend and is able to guide you through all kinds of tough situations. Unlike human friends, who sometimes let you down, he will be loyal, sticking with you through everything.

As with human friends, this relationship is a two-way street. You need to be a friend in return. You need to invest some of yourself— your time, your energy, your attention—in order to strengthen this friendship with God's Spirit. As with a human friendship, the payoff is worth it. With the Spirit as your constant companion, you might feel lonely sometimes, but you will never be alone.

My Prayer

Dear God,
I welcome your Spirit into my life. Please show me how I can be a better friend to your Spirit and solidify this relationship.
Amen.

Stone
for the Journey

God's Spirit is an amazing friend.

Final Word

His Spirit joins with our spirit to affirm that we are God's children. And since we are his children, we are his heirs. In fact, together with Christ we are heirs of God's glory. But if we are to share his glory, we must also share his suffering.

Romans 8:16–17 NLT

Be Prepared

> *Two men will be in the field. One will be taken, and the other will be left. Two women will be grinding grain with a mill. One will be taken, and the other will be left.*
>
> Matthew 24:40–41 NCV

The Boy Scout motto is "Be prepared." You might wonder, *How exactly? And be prepared for what?* A well-trained scout would answer, "Be prepared for anything." Is that even possible? If you're taking a hike in the woods, you'd probably want to pack things like a compass or a tracking device, drinking water, energy food, proper clothing, and maybe matches. A cell phone might come in handy too. But that's only enough preparation for a day hike. What about preparing for a life?

That calls for a different kind of preparedness, one that's even more important—spiritual preparedness. Let's face it, someone might be all ready for an earthquake or hurricane. But even with a well-stocked pantry, a generator, a tank of drinking water, medicine and first-aid items, candles, blankets, and other emergency supplies, that person could still be caught off guard if, instead of a natural disaster, there was a spiritual disaster.

Jesus says he will come to earth in the last days to gather up those who believe in him—the ones whose hearts are ready for his return—and take them back to heaven with him. But the ones who don't believe—even if they have everything necessary to survive floods and famines—will be left in the lurch when they realize their lack of spiritual preparedness.

While it's good to be prepared for any kind of emergency, it's even better to be prepared to hear and respond to Jesus when he calls out to you. When he says it's time to go, be ready.

My Prayer

Dear God,
Help me to be spiritually prepared. I know that means I need to stay connected to you. Thank you for your promise to see me through whatever comes my way.
Amen.

Stone
for the Journey

God prepares me for what lies ahead.

Final Word

We do not lose heart. Though our outer self is wasting away, our inner self is being renewed day by day.

2 Corinthians 4:16 ESV

46

Hold On!

Words from the Rock

I have told you these things so that you won't aban-
don your faith. For you will be expelled from the
synagogues, and the time is coming when those
who kill you will think they are doing a holy service
for God. This is because they have never known
the Father or me. Yes, I'm telling you these things
now, so that when they happen, you will remember
my warning. I didn't tell you earlier because I was
going to be with you for a while longer.

John 16:1–4 NLT

*J*esus knew that his disciples were going to go through a
kind of living hell after he was gone. His beloved followers would be beaten and tortured and imprisoned and even killed
because of their relationship with him. In essence, they would be
brutally terrorized in an attempt to completely shut down Chris-
tianity. Some evil leaders wanted Jesus's message stopped in its tracks,
and they mistakenly thought they could accomplish their diabolical

plan by persecuting and eliminating anyone who followed Jesus. Of course, they were wrong.

Jesus never tried to hide these frightening facts from his followers. He was blunt with them—so much so that if their faith had been weak, some of them might have slunk away like dogs with their tails between their legs. Really, how appealing would it be to hear that not only were you going to be bullied, tortured, and possibly murdered, but as a result, your loved ones would probably suffer as well? The forecast was grim.

Perhaps some might have preferred not to know what was coming—they might have thought ignorance was bliss. But Jesus wanted them to know so that they wouldn't be surprised or taken aback and they could hold tight to their faith. He knew that, more than anything, their faith was what would see them through.

It's no different for you. While you probably will never be treated as badly as his disciples were, you will go through tough times. Sometimes you might even suffer for your beliefs, but ultimately, if you hold on to Jesus, you will make it through. When you get hit with something hard, see it as a reminder to cling to your faith—and hold on tight!

My Prayer

Dear God,
Instead of getting rattled and worried when hard times come my way, please remind me that I need to hold on to you more tightly.
Amen.

Stone
for the Journey

Tough challenges call for tough faith.

Final Word

Don't blame God when you are tempted! God cannot be tempted by evil, and he doesn't use evil to tempt others.

James 1:13 CEV

47

Always Ready

Be on your guard! You don't know when your Lord will come. Homeowners never know when a thief is coming, and they are always on guard to keep one from breaking in. Always be ready! You don't know when the Son of Man will come.

Matthew 24:42–44 CEV

No one ever plans to be robbed. Even if you hear that there's a thief in the neighborhood, you can't predict if he'll hit your house tonight or tomorrow night or next week. In most burglaries, the victims are caught unawares and taken completely by surprise. So a lot of homeowners use home security systems for protection, because even if it's the middle of the night and you're sleeping and unaware of a break-in, a security system is on top of it. A security system never sleeps. That is, unless someone forgets to turn it on. Then there's a problem.

Here Jesus is reminding you to make sure you keep your spiritual security system up and running and in good shape. That means you don't neglect things like prayer or reading your Bible or spending time with other believers. To neglect those habits is to neglect your spiritual security system—and that leaves you vulnerable.

When you're doing what you should—maintaining your spiritual security system—you are ready for anything. And that brings a special sense of peace—the kind of peace that lets you enjoy a good night's sleep without worrying about a break-in. You can rest easy because you know you've done what needs to be done.

Jesus wants you to be ready—not just for when he comes back to get you, but for every good thing he has for you until then. Be ready!

My Prayer

Dear God,
Help me to take responsibility for maintaining my spiritual security system by obeying you. I want to be ready for everything and anything, especially for you.
Amen.

Stone
for the Journey

God wants me to be ready for whatever comes my way.

Final Word

You must learn to endure everything, so that you will be completely mature and not lacking in anything.

James 1:4 CEV

48

Change Is Good

Words from the Rock

Now I am going to him who sent me, yet none of you asks me, "Where are you going?" Because I have said these things, you are filled with grief. But I tell you the truth: It is for your good that I am going away. Unless I go away, the Counselor will not come to you; but if I go, I will send him to you.

John 16:5–7 NIV

Some people don't like change. They resist anything different and want everything to remain the same—status quo, leave it be, don't rock the boat. . . . But change is inevitable. Like it or not, change happens. For the most part, it's a good thing, even if you can't understand it at the time.

However, as the end of Jesus's earthly life drew closer, his disciples were not eager for change. They did not want to lose Jesus—they felt they needed him and that he still had work to do with them and others. And they most certainly did not want to see him die. What possible good could come of that? No, Jesus's followers longed for him to remain with them on earth indefinitely. They loved him and knew that life had never been as wonderful or exciting or fulfilling as it was with Jesus around. If his disciples had called the shots, Jesus never would have left them. Fortunately for everyone, God had other plans.

If Jesus had remained with his disciples and all had stayed the same, God's plan for forgiveness and redemption would have been thwarted. Jesus had to die on the cross and come back to life in order to change things. That was God's intention all along, and Jesus knew it. He also knew that he couldn't send his Spirit back to help his believers unless he first left. They were going to need his Spirit so they could be changed and mature.

Jesus wants the same for you. He wants his Spirit to change you—to help you grow and become more like him. Change really is good!

My Prayer

Dear God,
Thank you for your perfect plan. Thank you for sending your Spirit to change me. Please help me to be more like you.
Amen.

Stone
for the Journey

God's changes in me are good.

Final Word

Come on, let's leave the preschool fingerpainting exercises on Christ and get on with the grand work of art. Grow up in Christ.

Hebrews 6:1 Message

49

When No One's Looking

Words from the Rock

*Who then is the faithful and wise servant, whom
the master has put in charge of the servants in his
household to give them their food at the proper time?
It will be good for that servant whose master finds
him doing so when he returns. I tell you the truth,
he will put him in charge of all his possessions.*

Matthew 24:45–47 NIV

Have you ever walked into a fast-food restaurant or small
business and seen that the employees are slacking?
Maybe someone is talking on a cell phone and someone else is sitting on a counter, and you wait for them to come help you, but it's
like they don't care. Maybe they're thinking, *We only make minimum
wage—what's the big deal?* But what would happen if the owner of
the business walked in? They'd probably snap right to it. Well, unless
they wanted to get fired.

Some people act differently based on who is watching them. For instance, students don't usually cheat if the teacher has her eyes on them. Children don't sneak candy if Mom is nearby. But what happens when no one is looking?

Jesus describes an employee who does what's expected even though the employer is far away. This is a worker who knows what needs doing and enjoys doing it. This employee probably gets satisfaction from doing things right. And when the employer returns, he's pleasantly surprised. He feels fortunate to have such a good worker and rewards him or her for a job well done.

How do you behave when you think no one is looking? Do you slack off, break rules, or do what you know you shouldn't? Or do you get satisfaction from doing things right even if it seems like no one but you can see? And how does it feel to remember that God is always watching? He misses nothing. God wants you to grow up so that you'll do what's right no matter who's looking. Why is that? Because he knows that is what's best for you and will make you happiest, and he plans to reward you for it.

My Prayer

Dear God,
Please teach me to do what's right no matter who is watching me. Help me to remember that it's really in my best interest to obey you.
Amen.

Stone
for the Journey

God knows and rewards when I obey.

Final Word

Then you will not become spiritually dull and indifferent. Instead, you will follow the example of those who are going to inherit God's promises because of their faith and endurance.

Hebrews 6:12 NLT

Perceptions

Words from the Rock

> When he comes, he'll expose the error of the godless world's view of sin, righteousness, and judgment: He'll show them that their refusal to believe in me is their basic sin; that righteousness comes from above, where I am with the Father, out of their sight and control; that judgment takes place as the ruler of this godless world is brought to trial and convicted.
>
> John 16:8–11 Message

Most of the human race shares a common flaw in the area of perception—we think our point of view is correct. As a result, we can be quick to jump to wrong conclusions and make false assumptions. We form opinions on things we don't understand. We pass judgment without knowledge. It's just the human way. But it's not God's way.

A great part of Jesus's earthly mission was to show us a different way to think and reason. He basically wanted to shake things up.

Whether because of old, preconceived notions about religion or a misunderstanding of the nature of God, Jesus wanted to reform our hearts and minds.

Before Jesus came to earth, much of the religious community attempted to keep God in a box. They allowed their own human restrictions to limit their perception of him. But Jesus broke that box wide open. He showed people different sides of God—like forgiveness, compassion, mercy, and love. Jesus's life revealed that God was a lot different than many had assumed.

Unfortunately, we sometimes fall back to our old human ways—making wrong assumptions about God. Maybe we decide God is angry or mean. Or we conclude that he can't possibly love everyone—what about serial killers? Or we deduce that God's forgiveness is something we can earn or deserve. That's when we need to return to Jesus—we need to focus on his words and his teaching and allow him to transform our earthly minds so we can think and reason more like him.

My Prayer

Dear God,
I confess that sometimes I make snap judgments and come to wrong conclusions. Please change my thinking to be more like yours.
Amen.

Stone
for the Journey

God can transform my thinking.

Final Word

Don't be like the people of this world, but let God change the way you think. Then you will know how to do everything that is good and pleasing to him.

Romans 12:2 CEV

Responsible Faith

Words from the Rock

The kingdom of heaven is like what happened one night when ten girls took their oil lamps and went to a wedding to meet the groom. Five of the girls were foolish and five were wise. The foolish ones took their lamps, but no extra oil. The ones who were wise took along extra oil for their lamps. . . .

While the foolish girls were on their way to get some oil, the groom arrived. The girls who were ready went into the wedding, and the doors were closed. Later the other girls returned and shouted, "Sir, sir! Open the door for us!"

But the groom replied, "I don't even know you!"

So, my disciples, always be ready! You don't know the day or the time when all this will happen.

Matthew 25:1–4, 10–13 CEV

Imagine that you're on your way to your best friend's wedding and you need to be on time because you're in the bridal party. It's a long road trip across a barren desert, and your small car is packed full with four other bridal party members, as well as their things. Since this is a big wedding, there's another car packed full of wedding party members driving the same route.

As you're topping off your gas tank at the last gas station on the edge of the desert, you notice the driver of the other car in the convenience store buying snacks but not filling her tank. You remind her that she needs to gas up, but she just laughs and says, "Don't be such a worrywart. We're fine." You warn her she could run out of gas, but she just blows you off. Worried you might be late, you head out.

Midway through the desert, your cell phone rings—the other car has run out of gas and wants your help. But what can you do? Your car's already packed full. You don't have gas to spare. If you go back, everyone will miss the wedding. Sad as it is, you have to keep going and let them figure it out.

The point of this story? The gas symbolizes faith. You are responsible to fill up your own tank. You can warn someone, but you can't fill up their tank with your faith. They must have their own or suffer the consequences.

My Prayer

Dear God,
I realize that I'm responsible for maintaining my own faith. I want to take this seriously. Help me to keep my tank full.
Amen.

Stone
for the Journey

God expects me to maintain my faith.

Final Word

This is my prayer: that your love may abound more and more in knowledge and depth of insight, so that you may be able to discern what is best and may be pure and blameless until the day of Christ, filled with the fruit of righteousness that comes through Jesus Christ—to the glory and praise of God.

Philippians 1:9–11 NIV

Timing Is Everything

Words from the Rock

I have much more to say to you, but right now it would be more than you could understand. The Spirit shows what is true and will come and guide you into the full truth. The Spirit doesn't speak on his own. He will tell you only what he has heard from me, and he will let you know what is going to happen.

John 16:12–13 CEV

It's easy to get in a hurry, to feel rushed—like you're racing the clock. With "help" from instant messaging, high-speed internet service, fast-food chains . . . it almost seems like the world is spinning faster and faster. As a result, we can get into the habit of expecting things to move quickly, and we become irritated when something takes longer than we think it should. We want what we want, and we want it now!

But there can be good reasons to wait. For instance, if you're baking a cake, it won't do any good to rush the cooking time. Taking it out of the oven too soon will ruin it.

Spiritual things can be like that too. Jesus has a lot to tell you, to teach you, and to show you, but he knows you can handle only so much at once. To dump everything on you would totally overwhelm you. That's why Jesus wants his Spirit to dwell in you. The Spirit knows when it's time to show you certain things. He knows when it's the opportune moment to push you in a particular direction, and when it's just the right instant to warn you to avoid something.

Hopefully you're tuned in and your spiritual watch isn't running too fast or too slow. With God's Spirit, timing is everything. To rush the Spirit isn't just futile, it's foolish—not to mention impossible since you can't hurry God. Waiting on God diligently and patiently will accomplish far more than trying to speed things up. Trust God enough to slow down and listen.

My Prayer

Dear God,
I know I can be impatient and want to hurry things up. Show me how to align my spiritual clock with yours. Teach me to tune in to your Spirit.
Amen.

Stone
for the Journey

God's timing is perfect.

Final Word

He will keep you strong to the end so that you will be free from all blame on the day when our Lord Jesus Christ returns.

1 Corinthians 1:8 NLT

Full Disclosure

Words from the Rock

*The Spirit of truth will bring glory to me, because
he will take what I have to say and tell it to you.
All that the Father has is mine. That is why I said
that the Spirit will take what I have to say and
tell it to you.*

John 16:14–15 NCV

Everyone has seen news flashes. Maybe they're text messages
or blurbs on TV or headlines on the internet. They might be
something shocking or sensational, like a jetliner went down, a rock
star died, or there's been a shooting. You're given just enough information to pique your interest. Naturally, you want to find out
more, and as you investigate, you might discover that the news event
is so recent that you can't get to the bottom of it. You might even
be getting false information. Or you could find out that the story's
been way overblown just to get you to tune in to some irresponsible
news source.

It's not like that with Jesus. Because God has made everything known to him, he likewise wants to make everything known to you. Jesus wants you to understand things like God's love and forgiveness, how important it is to obey him, and God's plan for your life. He can do this through his Spirit. Of course, he won't do it all at once since that would blow your mind. But he will inform you of what you need when you need it. You can trust that his revelations will be honest and accurate.

Your responsibility is to stay tuned in to him. Instead of listening to unreliable sources—ones that may or may not be right—you need to make sure you're getting your information from God's sources, via things like the Bible, God's Spirit, or wise and trusted counsel. You can trust that, in the right timing—when you stay connected and obedient—what you need to know will be made known to you. You will not be misled or left in the dark because Jesus promises to give you full disclosure.

My Prayer

Dear God,
I want to know your plans for my life. Thank you for promising to reveal to me what I need to know. Help me to stay tuned in to your Spirit.
Amen.

Stone
for the Journey

God's Spirit keeps me informed so I can follow him.

Final Word

God was kind and decided that Christ would choose us to be God's own adopted children.

Ephesians 1:5 CEV

Eternal Investment

Words from the Rock

[Before going on a long trip, a businessman asked his employees to supervise some investments.] To one he gave five thousand dollars, to another two thousand, to a third one thousand, depending on their abilities. Then he left. Right off, the first employee went to work and doubled his employer's investment. The second did the same. But the man with the single thousand dug a hole and carefully buried his employer's money.

After a long absence, the employer of those three employees came back and settled up with them. The one given five thousand dollars showed him how he had doubled his investment. His employer commended him: "Good work! You did your job well. From now on be my partner."

The employee with the two thousand showed how he also had doubled his employer's investment. His employer commended him: "Good work! You did your job well. From now on be my partner."

Matthew 25:14–23 Message*

---

*In this passage, "servant" and "master" have been replaced with "employee" and "employer" respectively.

*I*n some ways, belonging to God is like being part of a family business. Jesus tells this story to explain how it works. God is the head of this business, and although he doesn't give us all the exact same things to work with, he gives us exactly what we need to succeed. For starters, he gives us our minds and our bodies, but beyond that, he gives us different skills. One person might be talented at speaking, another might have a gift of helping out, and another might be a great listener. God considers all the varied abilities to be equally important. The question is, what do we do with them?

God wants you to be like the first two employees in the story—to use whatever he's given you to the best of your ability. He wants you to step out of your comfort zone, take a few risks, go to some extremes, and live your life fully, trusting him to get you where you need to go. That's when there's a big payoff.

What kind of talent has God given you? How are you using it? Are you partnering with God? Or are you burying your gift in a dark hole? If you trust God, you'll want to step up and take your skills to the next level.

My Prayer

Dear God,
I do want to trust you more. Even if it makes me uncomfortable, help me to do something great with what you've given me so I can honor you with a big payoff!
Amen.

Stone
for the Journey

**God's gifts
are meant
to be used.**

Final Word

We have different gifts, according to the grace given us. If a man's gift is prophesying, let him use it in proportion to his faith.

Romans 12:6 NIV

55

Coward's Reward

Words from the Rock

The employee given one thousand said, "[Boss], I know you have high standards and hate careless ways, that you demand the best and make no allowances for error. I was afraid I might disappoint you, so I found a good hiding place and secured your money. Here it is, safe and sound down to the last cent."

The employer was furious. "That's a terrible way to live! It's criminal to live cautiously like that! If you knew I was after the best, why did you do less than the least? The least you could have done would have been to invest the sum with the bankers, where at least I would have gotten a little interest.

"Take the thousand and give it to the one who risked the most. And get rid of this 'play-it-safe' who won't go out on a limb. Throw him out into utter darkness."

Matthew 25:24–30 Message*

---

* In this passage, "servant" and "master" have been replaced with "employee" and "employer" respectively.

*F*aith is not fearful. How does that employee sound to you? Can't you just hear his quavering voice? Can't you imagine him cowering down in front of his employer? He's whining and complaining like he thinks his generous employer (the one who'd entrusted him with a lot of money) is a big bully. How would that make the employer feel? Here he'd trusted this guy, and what he gets in return is cowardly criticism. It's as if the employee is blaming the employer for his own bad judgment.

Naturally, the employer is going to be frustrated. What good is an employee like that? He gives the guy something to work with, and the foolish employee digs a hole in the dirt and buries it. What is up with that?

That's how Jesus describes us if we don't use the life God has given us. We only get one go-round on earth, and if we're so fearful and distrustful that we don't live it to the fullest—if we don't utilize all that God has entrusted us with—we might as well dig a hole and jump into it.

My Prayer

Dear God,
Show me how to live my life to the fullest. I want to use all you've given me, believing that you have big plans and trusting you to bring them to pass.
Amen.

Stone
for the Journey

I will live large for God.

Final Word

Always be full of joy in the Lord. I say it again—rejoice! Let everyone see that you are considerate in all you do. Remember, the Lord is coming soon.

Philippians 4:4–5 NLT

Before the Dawn

Words from the Rock

Are you trying to figure out among yourselves what
I meant when I said, "In a day or so you're not going
to see me, but then in another day or so you will
see me"? Then fix this firmly in your minds: You're
going to be in deep mourning while the godless
world throws a party. You'll be sad, very sad, but
your sadness will develop into gladness.

John 16:19–20 Message

*Y*ou've probably heard the saying, "It's darkest right before
the dawn." It's true—the world can seem like a cold, black
place when you're in the midst of a really difficult time. Whether
you're grieving a lost friendship, a broken heart, or even a death, the
world can feel hopeless and bleak.

Jesus knew his disciples were about to go through a rough period
like that. He knew they would feel lost, deserted, even in despair. But
he wanted them to understand it would only be temporary, that their

overwhelming sadness would be replaced with joy and gladness. He didn't want them to lose hope.

Jesus knows you'll have times like that in your life. Maybe they will never be as dark and discouraging as the three days his disciples spent thinking that the world as they knew it had ended, that the hope of the world had died on the cross. Still, Jesus is aware that your life won't always be smooth and easy. That's not how it is for anyone who chooses to follow him. He knows there will be ups and downs. There will be sad times and happy times. But the sun will always rise after a night of darkness and despair. In time, your joy will return . . . and someday you'll experience sunlight and joy forever.

My Prayer

Dear God,
I realize my earthly life isn't supposed to be nonstop sunshine and gladness. When times are dark, please remind me it won't always be like that.
Amen.

Stone
for the Journey

God replaces my darkness with light.

Final Word

If we live in the light, as God does, we share in life with each other. And the blood of his Son Jesus washes all our sins away.

1 John 1:7 CEV

57

Pain to Joy

Words from the Rock

> *Whenever a woman is in labor she has pain, because her hour has come; but when she gives birth to the child, she no longer remembers the anguish because of the joy that a child has been born into the world. Therefore you too have grief now; but I will see you again, and your heart will rejoice, and no one will take your joy away from you.*
>
> John 16:21–22 NASB

*T*here's nothing that Jesus doesn't understand. Although he never had a baby, he perfectly describes how a mother feels after giving birth to a child. Labor, no matter how short it is (and it's usually not), feels like it will never end. In fact, the actual birthing process is one of the most physically painful experiences a human can endure. Yet most mothers will tell you that as soon as the baby is safely delivered and nestled in her arms, she forgets all about the pain she just endured. It's like her brain is temporarily wiped clean.

Even when she does remember it later, it's as if the memory has been softened or diminished somehow. Otherwise there would be a lot fewer children in this world.

Jesus uses the childbirth metaphor to describe the enormous suffering his disciples will experience when he's temporarily removed from their world. Their grief will be excruciating—as painful as childbirth. But, he points out, it won't last long. When they reunite with Jesus, all that suffering will be forgotten.

Being separated from Jesus is supposed to hurt. It's God's way of reminding you to stay connected. If you experience that kind of intense spiritual anguish, the kind that aches deep inside, you need to do everything you can to reconnect yourself to Jesus. Once that relationship is restored, all sense of pain will fade away—it will be replaced with real joy!

My Prayer

Dear God,
I don't want anything to separate me from you.
If something does, help me to recognize it and repair it quickly.
Amen.

Stone
for the Journey

**I find joy
in Jesus.**

Final Word

Those who plant in tears will harvest with shouts of joy.

Psalm 126:5 NLT

Love in Action

58

Words from the Rock

The King will say . . . , "I was hungry, and you gave me food. I was thirsty, and you gave me something to drink. I was alone and away from home, and you invited me into your house. I was without clothes, and you gave me something to wear. I was sick, and you cared for me. I was in prison, and you visited me."

Then the good people will answer, "Lord, when did we see you hungry . . . thirsty . . . away from home . . . without clothes . . . sick or in prison?" . . .

Then the King will answer, "I tell you the truth, anything you did for even the least of my people here, you also did for me."

Matthew 25:34–40 NCV

It's not difficult to say the words "I love you." In fact, some people say these words rather carelessly, not really considering the meaning. There are others who say them insincerely, when they actually feel no love whatsoever. Some people even use them manipulatively, in order to get something from someone.

God wants your love for him to be genuine, and one way to show that love is real is by putting it into action. When you love someone, you're willing to go the distance to help them. If they're in need, you give. If they're lonely, you comfort. That's the way love acts.

Jesus takes this to an ever deeper level. He says we show our love to him in the way we love others. When we feed a hungry person, we feed Jesus. We give a poor person clothes, and it's like we clothed Jesus. We invite a homeless person into our home, and Jesus is there too. We visit an inmate, and Jesus feels we have visited him.

Nothing pleases Jesus more than when you go out of your way to love others selflessly and wholeheartedly like that. His Spirit will lead you and guide you in loving that way—if you're tuned in. Instead of just telling Jesus you love him, why not put it into action!

My Prayer

Dear God,
I do love you and want to show it by loving others. Please help me to see those in need and how I can help them.
Amen.

Stone
for the Journey

Love for others equals love for Jesus.

Final Word

Dear children, let's not merely say that we love each other; let us show the truth by our actions.

1 John 3:18 NLT

59

Just Ask

Words from the Rock

At that time you won't need to ask me for anything. I tell you the truth, you will ask the Father directly, and he will grant your request because you use my name. You haven't done this before. Ask, using my name, and you will receive, and you will have abundant joy.

John 16:23–24 NLT

Sometimes you'll hear someone say, "Just call me if you need anything." Sure, it sounds sweet and nice, and they might even mean it—or maybe they're just being polite. Would that friend sound as generous and kind if you called at three in the morning and asked him or her to come plunge your toilet? Probably not.

Jesus is not like that. And God never sleeps. When you are promised that you can ask for anything at any time—and that you will be heard and answered—you can believe it. Jesus gives you that kind of access to the Father because he's like your hotline to God. Does that mean you have a spiritual genie? That if you ask for something, your wish is his command and he'll give you whatever you want, like a new car or a million dollars or a singing career? If you think that, you're missing the point.

It's all about being connected to Jesus. When you're tight with Jesus, his Spirit will guide you so that you understand how to ask for what you need. You will know how to pray about what really matters—like helping people to know God better, ways you can grow in your faith, or anything else God wants to do in your life. As you get closer to Jesus, your prayers become more on target with what God wants.

My Prayer

Dear God,
Thank you for always being there and for hearing my prayers 24-7. I want to get closer to Jesus so I can pray the way you want me to. Amen.

Stone
for the Journey

Jesus teaches me to pray.

Final Word

We ought always to give thanks to God for you . . . because your faith is growing abundantly, and the love of every one of you for one another is increasing.

2 Thessalonians 1:3 ESV

60

Best of Both Worlds

Words from the Rock

> *I've used figures of speech in telling you these things. Soon I'll drop the figures and tell you about the Father in plain language. Then you can make your requests directly to him in relation to this life I've revealed to you.*
>
> John 16:25–26 Message

Do you remember what kinds of books you enjoyed when you were a young child? If you were like most kids, you liked the books with pictures. Big, fun, bright, colorful picture books. The best ones didn't have too many words—because as we all know, a picture is worth a thousand words. Maybe you had a favorite picture book, one you'd heard read so much that you could pretend to read, although you were simply reciting what you knew by heart from hearing it so much. That's part of childhood—and the first stage of learning to read.

In a way, those children's picture books are a bit like the stories Jesus told. Remember his parables? Those straightforward stories were created to help "early learners" understand God's kingdom better, and simple enough that they were easy to memorize. All that was for good reason, because Jesus didn't want to overwhelm everyone with too much information. Yet he knew the time would come when he wouldn't need to paint so many word pictures. He anticipated the day when he'd speak to his followers in a whole new grown-up way.

Jesus looks forward to the same thing with you. The more time you spend with Jesus, the more you know about him and the Bible, the more you'll become like him. As a result, you'll have a better grasp of some hard-to-understand concepts. But here's the best part—because Jesus also wants us to remain childlike in ways, you'll probably always love the "picture book" parables too. It's like the best of both worlds.

My Prayer

Dear God,
Thank you for communicating to me on a level I can understand. I appreciate the fact that, more than anything, you want me to know you better.
Amen.

Stone
for the Journey

God speaks my language.

Final Word

If we seem out of our minds, it is between God and us. But if we are in our right minds, it is for your good.

2 Corinthians 5:13 CEV

61

Love Connection

*God the Father loves you because you love me,
and you believe that I have come from him. I came
from the Father into the world, but I am leaving
the world and returning to the Father.*

John 16:27–28 CEV

*J*esus can't make things any clearer than he does here. This is plain-speak at its best. This clear statement is all about love and connection. Jesus's love connects us to the Father's love—and then Jesus returns to the Father. Can it get any simpler than that? Yet if you know anything about religion and history and humankind, you know that it's still possible for people to mess up this truth.

In fact, in the two thousand years since Jesus gave this statement, many religious leaders have tried to complicate its simple message. Some have tried to make it seem that this love relationship must be earned or that forgiveness must be purchased. Others have portrayed Jesus's love as exclusive—like it's a special club with a secret handshake—and that it's okay to push others away. Some have twisted Jesus's message, completely deleting the love part, in order to hurt and even kill others.

Jesus's message of love and acceptance is so simple and straightforward, so accessible and pure . . . yet some still manage to mangle it. What can you do to keep that from happening to you? What can you do to ensure that you don't get pulled down the wrong trail? How about writing Jesus's words on your heart? Memorize some Bible verses that are meaningful to you so that you can take them with you wherever you go. That way if you run into someone who wants to point you in another direction, you won't be misled. Perhaps you can even help them return to the truth!

My Prayer

Dear God,
Thanks for the simplicity of the love connection. Help me to keep that connection alive and vital and to write your words on my heart.
Amen.

Stone
for the Journey

Jesus's love connects me to God.

Final Word

You are the body of Christ, and each one of you is a part of it.

1 Corinthians 12:27 NIV

62

Coming Back

Words from the Rock

> *Do you finally believe? In fact, you're about to make a run for it—saving your own skins and abandoning me. But I'm not abandoned. The Father is with me. I've told you all this so that trusting me, you will be unshakable and assured, deeply at peace. In this godless world you will continue to experience difficulties. But take heart! I've conquered the world.*
>
> John 16:31–33 Message

*P*eople don't always do what is right. They don't always act like they know they should. Jesus's disciples—the same men who later founded the original Christian church, shared the gospel with thousands, even gave up their lives for their faith—were no different. When the going got tough . . . they actually ran the other direction.

Frightened and confused, these men cowered in dark corners, considered abandoning their faith, and even denied knowing Jesus, just as he had predicted they would do. That's why he told them ahead of time what would happen—to reassure them that it would be okay.

Jesus understands your human weakness. He knows you can't possibly live the "perfect Christian life" day in and day out. He knows you'll blow it. But he wants you to realize that, even when you do blow it, he's ready to welcome you back. Because of who he is (he never blew it), he has made up for all your shortcomings, and he is able to forgive you and get you back on track.

Even though you'll feel sad and discouraged when you turn your back on Jesus, you shouldn't beat yourself up too much. Remember that Jesus understands. Most of all he wants you to return to him— to confess you blew it, to receive his forgiveness, and to believe he is able to restore your relationship with him. He wants to bring you back to that place of peace.

My Prayer

Dear God,
I'm relieved that you know I'm not perfect and that I'll blow it sometimes. Help me to be quick to turn back to you. Thank you for welcoming me with open arms!
Amen.

Stone
for the Journey

God's love always welcomes me back.

Final Word

Therefore confess your sins to each other and pray for each other so that you may be healed. The prayer of a righteous man is powerful and effective.

James 5:16 NIV

63

Like a River

"I was hungry, and you gave me nothing to eat. I was thirsty, and you gave me nothing to drink. I was alone and away from home, and you did not invite me into your house. I was without clothes, and you gave me nothing to wear. I was sick and in prison, and you did not care for me."

Then those people will answer, "Lord, when did we see you hungry or thirsty or alone and away from home or without clothes or sick or in prison? When did we see these things and not help you?" . . .

"Anything you refused to do for even the least of my people here, you refused to do for me."

Matthew 25:42–45 NCV

Some people think that the more they keep for themselves, the richer they will be. Maybe that makes sense on some levels. But have you ever seen hoarders—people who refuse to get rid of anything? Their houses fill up until they can barely walk through the rooms or use the furniture. Yet many of them will go out and get even more stuff—hauling it in and piling it up until it's truly a health hazard and firetrap. This kind of behavior seems crazy to most people, but a hoarder thinks it's normal.

There are a lot of explanations for hoarders. Some reasons are complicated, but others are common—like insecurity, fear of poverty, or anxiety that they'll run out of something or need something they've given away. In a way, it's like not believing that God can and will provide for them. Instead of relying on God's generosity, they are grabbing as much as they can and stuffing it into their homes. Not only is it impairing and dysfunctional, it's exactly the opposite of how God wants us to live.

God generously gives us what we need, and he wants us to be just as generous to those around us—especially to those in need. God knows that when we give, we open ourselves up to receive. Like a river that needs to flow freely to stay healthy, we need to give freely to stay healthy. When we bless others with our generosity, it's like we're blessing Jesus.

My Prayer

Dear God,
Please show me ways I can be generous.
Whether it's with my time or my money or my friendship, let me give to others like I'm giving to you.
Amen.

Stone
for the Journey

God wants his generosity to flow through me.

Final Word

[If one's gift] is contributing to the needs of others, let him give generously . . . let him do it cheerfully.

Romans 12:8 NIV

64

With Open Arms

Words from the Rock

Father, the time has come for you to bring glory to your Son, in order that he may bring glory to you. And you gave him power over all people, so that he would give eternal life to everyone you give him.

John 17:1–2 CEV

efore Jesus came to earth, most religions were extremely exclusive. Remember how the scribes and Pharisees and religious leaders seemed to do everything possible to keep ordinary people from getting close to God? It was as if they felt it was their job to build a giant wall around God, posting signs that said "Keep Out" or "No Trespassing" or "Stay Away." There were other religions that weren't much different, as if religion was a private club—for members only. They had to pay their dues, be born in a certain family, obey certain rules, act a certain way, or live in a certain neighborhood just to be good enough to belong.

But Jesus said, "Enough!" Fed up with man-made efforts to separate people from God, Jesus was done with exclusivity. He opened his arms wide, inviting anyone and everyone to come and receive him. Then with arms still spread wide, he died on the cross so that God would welcome all believers into his kingdom. Unlike the other uptight religions, Jesus's rules were simple—love God and love others, and come on along!

When Jesus said he came for "all people" and for "everyone," he meant it. His love is not limited, and his mercy is endless. And he wants you to be an extension of his love and mercy to everyone around you. No walls. No barriers. No cliques. No exclusions. This is a party where everyone is invited. All are welcome. The way you show that you belong to Jesus is by inviting others into your life— with open arms!

My Prayer

Dear God,
Thank you for welcoming me into your family. Help me to be warm and inviting to everyone around me. I don't want to exclude anyone. Amen.

Stone
for the Journey

God welcomes me so I can welcome others.

Final Word

Love each other with genuine affection, and take delight in honoring each other.

Romans 12:10 NLT

65

Attention!

> As you know, the Passover is two days away—
> and the Son of Man will be handed over to be
> crucified.
>
> Matthew 26:2 NIV

*T*here was a time in Jesus's ministry when even his closest followers had no idea that his life would end so tragically. Maybe if they'd known that he was going to be sentenced to death like a common criminal, they would have hung their heads and slunk away. Perhaps Jesus knew this, and that was why he waited until his arrest and death were only hours away to speak so explicitly to his disciples. He knew they could bear only so much. He wanted to protect them from what he knew could be their undoing.

From the disciples' perspective, death was a permanent state of being. Jesus knew his friends would see this as his final exit—the end of the story, that's all there is. Yet he understood they needed to know what was coming—they needed to be privy to this shocking news so that, in time, they would understand.

Death is hard for anyone to grasp. Even if we believe in Jesus's promise of heaven and life after death, it's still painful and sad to see someone die. It cuts us to the core—and it really does feel final. Nothing on earth is more extreme than death. To experience that kind of a loss is like the ultimate wake-up call. No matter our state of mind, death always gets our attention.

Jesus knew that his death would get a lot of attention too, and when he rose from the dead, he would get even more. His victory over death would be one more thing to separate him from every other religion's leaders, one more thing to show that he was truly from God—the real deal. He died and rose so we can live. It's an amazing gift that should hold our attention for all of eternity.

My Prayer

Dear God,
Death does get my attention. Thank you for giving up everything so I can live. Help me to appreciate this today.
Amen.

Stone
for the Journey

Jesus's death gave me life.

Final Word

We believe that Jesus died and rose again and so we believe that God will bring with Jesus those who have fallen asleep in him.

1 Thessalonians 4:14 NIV

Jesus's Gift

Words from the Rock

This is eternal life: that people know you, the only true God, and that they know Jesus Christ, the One you sent.

John 17:3 NCV

*N*othing was more important to Jesus than for everyone to know his Father God. Nothing. And Jesus was willing to do anything to bring this message to everyone on earth. Anything.

Imagine it's a thousand years ago and you live in a fabulous kingdom with your wonderful father, and life is extremely good. You are surrounded by dear friends, and there is amazing food, beautiful gardens, swimming pools, horses to ride . . . It's the best place in the world. But this kingdom is surrounded by a moat of toxic liquid that will dissolve anything that touches it. This liquid was put there by people who dwell outside of the kingdom. Because you have a telescope, you know that the people on the other side are sick and starving, and thanks to earthquakes their land is being destroyed.

You tell your father you want to rescue them, so he lets you build a bridge over the moat.

You get to the other side and begin telling the people about your father. But their reactions are mixed. Some don't believe you—they say it's impossible to cross that moat. Some say your father is evil. Some ignore you or laugh at you. Finally, as their world is falling apart, you convince some to follow you back across the bridge, but as you get there you see the bridge is starting to dissolve. Quickly you stretch yourself across the bridge and tell people to just walk over you—and hurry to the other side. They make it, but in the process you fall into the toxic liquid and die.

That's kind of like what Jesus did for you. He gave up everything when he left his Father's kingdom. Then he laid down his life so you could meet his Father. That was his mission—his gift for all mankind. What is your response to that gift?

My Prayer

Dear God,
Thank you so much for sending Jesus. Thank you that Jesus was willing to die for me. Please help me to never take that gift for granted. Amen.

Stone
for the Journey

Jesus gave all for me to know God.

Final Word

Christ Jesus, who died—more than that, who was raised to life—is at the right hand of God and is also interceding for us.

Romans 8:34 NIV

67

Incomprehensible

Words from the Rock

> *I glorified You on the earth, having accomplished the work which You have given Me to do. Now, Father, glorify Me together with Yourself, with the glory which I had with You before the world was.*
>
> John 17:4–5 NASB

*I*t's hard to envision someplace you've never been before. Especially if you don't have photos or videos or some other kind of description. Even if someone tells you about this distant place, unless you have an astonishing imagination, you probably won't get it right.

When it comes to imagining how fantastic heaven is, no one on earth can possibly get it right. You could take all the very best things on earth (gorgeous mountains, white sandy beaches, majestic rain forests, stunning canyons, rolling fields of wildflowers, sapphire blue lakes—anything you think is beautiful), and even if you multiplied those wonders a thousand times, you'd still probably miss how incredible heaven really is. It's incomprehensible.

Even more incomprehensible is Jesus's willingness to leave heaven—and to leave his Father behind—in order to come to earth and complete the work God had set before him. Yet he did it—cheerfully, wholeheartedly, and selflessly. He threw everything he had into getting out the good news that God loved everyone and that he wanted a relationship with them. When Jesus's work was done, he took it a step further and gave up his own life in a brutal and humiliating death. What more could he do?

He did all this because of his love for his Father . . . and because of his love for you. With his mission complete, Jesus returned to heaven and was reunited with his Father. His reward for a job well done is to celebrate with everyone who's now welcome in heaven—including you! And if heaven was totally awesome before Jesus left, how much better it will be now!

My Prayer

Dear God,
Heaven really is incomprehensible, but I know it will be the best experience imaginable. I'm so thankful I'll get to participate in it.
Amen.

Stone
for the Journey

I cannot begin
to imagine
how fantastic
heaven is.

Final Word

Then I saw a new heaven and a new earth, for the first heaven and the first earth had passed away, and there was no longer any sea.

Revelation 21:1 NIV

68

All-Out Love

Why are you bothering this woman? She has done a beautiful thing to me. The poor you will always have with you, but you will not always have me. When she poured this perfume on my body, she did it to prepare me for burial. I tell you the truth, wherever this gospel is preached throughout the world, what she has done will also be told, in memory of her.

Matthew 26:10–13 NIV

One of Jesus's disciples appears to put more faith in money than he does in Jesus. Judas, the bookkeeper for the disciples, rants about a woman after she's emptied a very expensive bottle of perfume on Jesus. "Why this waste?" Judas demands. "We could've sold that perfume for a lot of money . . . and we could've even given the money to the poor."

Jesus knows this woman has done this extravagant thing out of pure selflessness. It's her way of expressing her love and gratitude to Jesus, who, as God's Son, isn't worried about something as insignificant as money. The most important thing here is that this woman understands who Jesus is—that he is part of God and that nothing is too good, too expensive, or too fine for him. Her gift is a form of true worship, and Jesus receives it as such. He even goes so far as to mention that this woman's gift will be used as an example of worship for years to come—and now, two thousand years later, we're reading about it!

How do you worship Jesus? Are you a cheapskate worshiper? Are you miserly in your praise? Do you hold back in fear that it costs too much to love him? Or do you realize that Jesus is King of Kings—and nothing is too good for him? Do you grasp that no matter how much praise and worship and love you lavish on him, it is no more than his due? Jesus invites you to pour yourself out like the woman with the perfume—holding nothing back!

My Prayer

Dear God,
I want to be like the woman with the perfume.
I want to pour myself out on you. Please teach me how to do that—to give my all like you did. Amen.

Stone
for the Journey

I will pour out my love for Jesus.

Final Word

Now we can rejoice in our wonderful new relationship with God because our Lord Jesus Christ has made us friends of God.

Romans 5:11 NLT

Family Ties

Words from the Rock

I have revealed you to the ones you gave me from this world. They were always yours. You gave them to me, and they have kept your word. Now they know that everything I have is a gift from you, for I have passed on to them the message you gave me. They accepted it and know that I came from you, and they believe you sent me.

John 17:6–8 NLT

*E*veryone has an innate longing to be part of a supportive, loving family. A few people are fortunate enough to enjoy a real sense of that kind of family here on earth. Maybe they're born into one, or they're adopted somewhere along the line. Or perhaps they figure out how to put together a family of their own making—a family of dear friends who are as close as blood relatives. Anyone who's included in a loving family appreciates its value and importance. Even those with slightly dysfunctional families probably wouldn't trade them in.

Yet for many people, and for many reasons, being part of a loving family is just a dream—an impossible dream. Some people live their entire lives feeling like they're on the outside looking in, and they experience loneliness whenever they see what appears to be a healthy and loving family.

God understands this. That's why it was so important for Jesus to come to earth and to accomplish his mission of introducing everyone to God. This was God's way to ensure that we all have a chance to be part of an incredibly, amazingly, miraculously loving family—his family. He gathers up all his children and welcomes us into his phenomenal family, and when the time is right, he brings us home to live with him and with Jesus throughout eternity. One great big happy family!

But it's even better than that—you can actually experience this sense of family right here and now. Once you become God's child, you're automatically linked to millions of spiritual brothers and sisters here on earth. You're no longer on the outside looking in—you are part of God's amazing family right now!

My Prayer

Dear God,
Thank you for adopting me into your incredible family. Help me to love my spiritual brothers and sisters the way you have loved me.
Amen.

Stone
for the Journey

I am part of God's family.

Final Word

By faith we have been made acceptable to God. And now, because of our Lord Jesus Christ, we live at peace with God.

Romans 5:1 CEV

Prayer Power

Words from the Rock

I pray for them. I am not praying for the world,
but for those you have given me, for they are yours.
All I have is yours, and all you have is mine. And
glory has come to me through them.

John 17:9–10 NIV

Sometimes it's hard to pray. We make all kinds of excuses. Like maybe you don't know quite what to say or how to say it. Maybe you wonder how long you should pray—is two minutes too short; is two hours too long? Perhaps you assume you need to get yourself to the right place to pray properly, like on a church pew or on your knees or on a mountaintop. Maybe you think you should read a book about prayer—just to make sure you're doing it correctly. It's even possible you've convinced yourself that you don't have the right kind of words to use in your prayers, that you need a special "spiritual" vocabulary that will make God sit up and listen.

Of course, that's all pretty ridiculous—because there are no rules for how to pray. Mostly God wants you to do it—just do it. Prayer is how you communicate with God. It's the way you express how you feel, what you need, what worries you. It's how you confess a problem or ask for help. It's how you thank God or tell him you love him. Prayer is like talking to a friend, and anytime is the right time to do it; anywhere is the right place. You don't even have to close your eyes or fold your hands or say, "Amen." In other words, prayer is quite simple. It's beneficial and something you need to do for your own health and well-being on a regular basis.

That's a lot to know about praying, but did you know that Jesus prays for you? Even though Jesus is God's Son and one with God, he still cares so much about you and loves you so much that he prays for you. That alone should convince you that prayer is vital. So what's stopping you from praying right now?

My Prayer

Dear God,
Show me how to pray to you. Remind me there are no rules. Help me to see that prayer is simply having a conversation with you.
Amen.

Stone
for the Journey

**God wants
to hear from
me today.**

Final Word

*I thank my God every time I remember you. In all
my prayers for all of you, I always pray with joy.*

Philippians 1:3–4 NIV

71

Lifetime Membership

Words from the Rock

I am no longer in the world; and yet they themselves are in the world, and I come to You. Holy Father, keep them in Your name, the name which You have given Me, that they may be one even as We are.

John 17:11 NASB

God designed us in a way that makes us long to be part of something bigger than ourselves. We desire a connected oneness—something that joins us into a larger community. Although some mistakenly assume that kind of connection can be accomplished through electronic means like text messaging, email, blogs, chat rooms, social networks, cell phones . . . what we actually want is something more—much, much more.

Maybe you've heard someone say, "It feels like something is missing in my life." Perhaps you've felt like that too—isolated, lonely, left out. Some people might become members of clubs or churches or cliques to find that connectedness. Others might gather at sports events or concerts, getting lost in the crowd and hoping that will substitute for belonging—until it's time to go home. A few might even take the dark route and join a gang. It's all about wanting to be included, to be a member of something, to belong.

Jesus knows about oneness because of his tight relationship with his Father—and all of heaven. He knows how important it is for everyone to participate in this kind of connection. He spent all of his earthly life trying to help us understand how much we need to unite ourselves to him and his Father. This doesn't mean you shouldn't belong to any other type of group. It simply means your most important membership—the one that will last for eternity—is in being connected to God. Jesus already paid your dues, so you might as well enjoy the privileges of membership.

My Prayer

Dear God,
Thank you for including me. Whenever I feel lonely or left out, please remind me that I belong to you.
Amen.

Stone
for the Journey

I have a lifetime membership with God.

Final Word

May our Lord Jesus Christ himself and God our Father, who loved us and by his grace gave us eternal encouragement and good hope, encourage your hearts and strengthen you in every good deed and word.

2 Thessalonians 2:16–17 NIV

Communion

Words from the Rock

> *Jesus . . . blessed the bread and broke it . . . and said, "Take this and eat it. This is my body."*
>
> *Jesus picked up a cup of wine and gave thanks to God . . . and said, "Take this and drink it. This is my blood, and with it God makes his agreement with you. It will be poured out, so that many people will have their sins forgiven. From now on I am not going to drink any wine, until I drink new wine with you in my Father's kingdom."*
>
> Matthew 26:26–29 CEV

Some call this event the Last Supper, and it's the final meal that Jesus ate before his death. What he says to his disciples during that meal is not only surprisingly graphic but also slightly disturbing on some levels. He tells them that they are eating his body and drinking his blood. But what does that mean? Certainly he's not endorsing cannibalism or vampirism.

The point Jesus is making is that he wants his followers to be so much a part of him, so connected to him, that it's as if his being (his flesh and blood) is actually inside each one of them—like his blood is flowing through their veins. That is real oneness. It's not easy to grasp, but Jesus knows it will take this kind of oneness for his followers to stick with him through all the trials and challenges that will soon be hurled at them. As graphic as the idea of eating his body and drinking his blood is, he wants to drive this concept home.

Jesus wants everyone to understand that his body will be beaten and broken and his blood will be spilled—in other words, he will die—in order to give us this kind of oneness with him. If we're repulsed by this truth, if we try to shove this gift away, we will miss out. As abhorrent as it might seem, it's only when we embrace Jesus's torturous death that we get to enjoy his forgiveness.

My Prayer

Dear God,
Thank you for dying on the cross, for being broken, and for spilling your blood so I can be one with you and receive your forgiveness and eternal life.
Amen.

Stone
for the Journey

Jesus's blood buys my forgiveness.

Final Word

Since we have now been justified by his blood, how much more shall we be saved from God's wrath through him!

Romans 5:9 NIV

73

Betrayal

While I was with them, I kept them safe by the power you have given me. I guarded them, and not one of them was lost, except the one who had to be lost. This happened so that what the Scriptures say would come true.

John 17:12 CEV

You probably know by now that one of Jesus's disciples is a betrayer. Judas Iscariot, the same man who was anxious about finances, sells Jesus out. He reveals Jesus's whereabouts for thirty pieces of silver. While this sounds diabolical and malicious, it's something that must happen in order to fulfill an old prophecy about Jesus. In order for people to understand that Jesus is truly the Messiah, the Son of God, all of the Old Testament prophecies must be fulfilled during Jesus's time on earth—and they are.

Jesus knows in advance he will be betrayed, and he's well aware that Judas will be responsible for turning him over to the authorities, after which Jesus will be beaten, interrogated, tortured, humiliated, and eventually killed. Yet Jesus loves Judas. He treats this betrayer as a dear friend. Right up until the end, when Judas reveals Jesus's identity with a kiss, Jesus never says a harsh word against him. We don't hear much about Judas after that—except that he is so grieved by his actions that he hangs himself.

We don't know whether or not Judas cried out to Jesus in his final breath, if he confessed his sin and begged for forgiveness . . . but it's possible that when we get to heaven we'll be surprised. We'll probably be surprised by a lot of things in heaven. But because we do know Jesus is all about mercy, love, and forgiveness, we can assume that Jesus would have reached out his hand to Judas.

In the same way, you can be assured that Jesus will forgive you when you betray him. And you will. Everyone betrays Jesus at some point in life. Whether it's briefly turning your back and pretending not to know him, or totally walking away from him for a while, you will betray him. The important thing is that you turn back to him, tell him you're sorry, and accept his forgiveness.

My Prayer

Dear God,
I don't ever want to betray you. If I do, please remind me that your forgiveness is there for me. Let me hurry back to you and confess that I blew it.
Amen.

Stone
for the Journey

God forgives the worst in me.

Final Word

God treats us much better than we deserve, and because of Christ Jesus, he freely accepts us and sets us free from our sins.

Romans 3:24 CEV

74

Wake Up!

Words from the Rock

> *[Jesus] prayed, saying, "My Father, if it is possible,*
> *let this cup pass from Me; yet not as I will, but*
> *as You will." And He came to the disciples and*
> *found them sleeping, and said to Peter, "So, you*
> *men could not keep watch with Me for one hour?*
> *Keep watching and praying that you may not enter*
> *into temptation; the spirit is willing, but the flesh*
> *is weak." He went away again a second time and*
> *prayed, saying, "My Father, if this cannot pass*
> *away unless I drink it, Your will be done."*
>
> Matthew 26:39–42 NASB

On the most difficult night of Jesus's life—which is about to end—at a time when he wants and needs his best friends (his beloved disciples) to surround him with their love and support . . . they are asleep. Jesus is desperately praying to his Father—confessing his concerns, expressing his deepest emotions, even to the point where he sweats drops of blood—and his buddies are snoozing.

It's as if the weight of the world . . . the entire universe . . . is resting on Jesus's shoulders tonight. He knows that his earthly mission (to save the human race) is nearly over. He's done everything possible to show them God's love and mercy—but is it enough? Time is running out, and his death is imminent. Because of his love for all mankind (then and now), he suffers great agony as he prays to the Father about what lies ahead. Then he submits his will to his Father, saying, "Do it your way, not mine." And throughout his torment, while he struggles, his friends are fast asleep.

It's tempting to take a nap when times get hard. It's like sleep is the great escape. While Jesus understands your humanity, he still warns you to be careful. He doesn't want your human weakness to cause you to fall flat on your face. Instead of dozing off when the going gets rough, why not go to Jesus and ask him for help? Wake up!

My Prayer

Dear God,
I confess that sometimes I want to hide from my problems. Remind me that you handle things differently. Help me to come to you for help.
Amen.

Stone
for the Journey

God wants me to face my troubles.

Final Word

We can rejoice, too, when we run into problems and trials, for we know that they help us develop endurance.

Romans 5:3 NLT

Complete Joy

Now I'm returning to you. I'm saying these things in the world's hearing so my people can experience my joy completed in them.

John 17:13 Message

*J*esus is talking to his Father about his friends and all the people who will follow him in the centuries to come—including you. Knowing his earthly time is nearly over, Jesus prays to his Father about what's to come. What will happen to his friends when he's gone? Although Jesus knows he's about to be killed, he's not even thinking about that. His primary concern is for his followers.

On a night when he knows that his earthly life is pretty much over, that he won't get to be with his friends anymore, that he won't get to heal and teach and do miracles, and that he is about to endure an excruciating form of death . . . he asks his Father to make sure his followers experience his joy.

Joy? On a dark, dismal night, when his buddies are fast asleep, while he is alone and suffering and in deep spiritual anguish, Jesus asks God to make sure his friends have joy? Yes. He's not only asking God to give them joy, he's asking God to *complete* his joy within them—in other words, to finish the work Jesus began.

He is entrusting his loved ones into his Father's hands because he knows that only God can finish this impossible mission. Only God can bring joy after what will soon become the darkest day in the history of the world. Jesus's faith in his Father convinces him that this is possible. Even now, Jesus knows that if his work is complete and full in you, it is because his Father has linked your life to his—which results in real joy.

My Prayer

Dear God,
Please complete Jesus's work in me so his joy will be part of my life. When I feel my joy is lacking, remind me to come to you.
Amen.

Stone
for the Journey

Jesus's joy in me means God is at work.

Final Word

Because of our faith, Christ has brought us into this place of undeserved privilege where we now stand, and we confidently and joyfully look forward to sharing God's glory.

Romans 5:2 NLT

76

Safekeeping

Words from the Rock

I have given them your word. And the world hates them because they do not belong to the world, just as I do not belong to the world. I'm not asking you to take them out of the world, but to keep them safe from the evil one. They do not belong to this world any more than I do.

John 17:14–16 NLT

*M*ore than anyone, Jesus understands that this world is a dangerous place. In fact, the eve of his murder is when he prays specifically for the safety of his friends. Their association with him puts them at serious risk. He already told them that if someone hated him, they will hate his disciples too—danger by association.

Jesus knows that this kind of danger and hatred will continue through the future—those who hate Jesus will hate anyone who belongs to him. That includes you—your association puts you at risk.

Because Jesus loves you just as much as he loved his disciples, he wants you to remain safe too.

Now, being that Jesus is the Son of God, you'd think he could do whatever it takes to keep you safe. If he wanted, he could probably design a special escape route, a secret passageway, that would swoosh you away from this earth to a secure location. But he doesn't want to do that. He would rather keep you safe in the midst of danger because he knows that's where you can be most effective.

Jesus doesn't want you to live an anxious, cautious, sheltered life. He doesn't want you cowering in corners, shivering in fear. Instead, he wants you to trust him and be assured of his ability to protect you as you face whatever comes your way. That kind of confidence gets attention—people see Jesus's power at work in you. That's when they want to find out how they can have this power for themselves.

My Prayer

Dear God,
I confess this world sometimes scares me, but I know you'll keep me safe. Help me to walk in that kind of confidence so others will see you in me.
Amen.

Stone
for the Journey

God will keep me safe.

Final Word

Something even greater than friendship is ours. Now that we are at peace with God, we will be saved by his Son's life.

Romans 5:10 CEV

77

Rags to Riches

Words from the Rock

Soon you will see the Son of Man sitting at the right side of God All-Powerful and coming on the clouds of heaven.

Matthew 26:64 CEV

*E*veryone enjoys a rags-to-riches story. Like when a homeless guy wins the lottery. Or someone rises up from the projects to stardom. Experiences like that get our attention and warm our hearts.

Jesus's life is the ultimate rags-to-riches tale. Actually, it's more like a riches-to-rags-to-riches story. First of all, he leaves all the riches and wonders and beauty of heaven to come to earth as a helpless baby. And he's not born in a hospital or even a house—no, Jesus is born in a lowly stable with farm animals watching.

Then, after Jesus spends his whole life serving others and doing God's will, he is captured and beaten and ridiculed and subjected to a brutal execution. Really, can a man's life end more miserably than that? Nailed to a cross between a couple of thieves while his executioners throw dice for his clothing, Jesus reaches an all-time low. Even though he trusts his Father, it must be difficult . . . and excruciatingly painful. And then he dies.

But here's the good part—the happy twist in the story that Jesus tells his disciples to anticipate. He wants them to realize that shortly after his death, he'll be alive again, and he'll be reunited with his Father. Jesus will have beaten death, and he will sit at God's right side. He will emerge from the depths of despair and rise up to join all the glories of heaven. There Jesus will rule and reign with his Father God. From rags to riches. And because of him, you will experience the same thing—your relationship with Jesus will transform your life from rags to riches!

My Prayer

Dear God,
I'm so thankful that no one and nothing could hold Jesus down. I know that his victory is my victory; his story is mine. I can go from rags to riches too.
Amen.

Stone
for the Journey

God can turn my life around.

Final Word

Could it be any clearer? Our old way of life was nailed to the cross with Christ, a decisive end to that sin-miserable life—no longer at sin's every beck and call!

Romans 6:6 Message

78

The Mission

Make them holy—consecrated—with the truth;
your word is consecrating truth. In the same way
that you gave me a mission in the world, I give
them a mission in the world. I'm consecrating my-
self for their sakes so they'll be truth-consecrated
in their mission.

John 17:17–19 Message

*J*esus's earthly mission is to spread the Good News—to communicate to the world that God loves everyone and wants them to be part of his family. Jesus passes that mission on to each of his friends. He invites every follower to imitate him in the mission of sharing that Good News. If you love Jesus, you won't want to let him down.

If you're like most people, though, you might find that mission a little overwhelming. How do you do it? Where do you begin? What if you fail? It's a big assignment, and it's pretty intimidating. Do you need some kind of special training? A college degree? Do you need to memorize the Bible from cover to cover first? What if someone questions your qualifications to do this mission?

Jesus doesn't ask you to do something he doesn't intend to help you with. He knows it's not easy. That's why he promises to send his Spirit to teach you. His Spirit of truth will show you how to share the Good News—he will guide you in how to tell others God loves them. Remember the two commandments Jesus gave you? Love God with all you are, and love your neighbor as yourself. If you do those two things, you will fulfill Jesus's mission, and others will notice you're living a life that stands out.

My Prayer

Dear God,
Thank you for giving me a mission. Thank you for sending your Spirit. Help me to keep your two commandments so I can fulfill your mission.
Amen.

Stone
for the Journey

My mission is to let God love others through me.

Final Word

It is by believing in your heart that you are made right with God, and it is by confessing with your mouth that you are saved.

Romans 10:10 NLT

Amazed by Grace

Words from the Rock

> Jesus said, "Father, forgive them, for they do not know what they are doing." . . .
>
> [A thief on the cross next to Jesus] said, "Jesus, remember me when you come into your kingdom."
>
> Jesus answered him, "I tell you the truth, today you will be with me in paradise."
>
> Luke 23:34, 42–43 NIV

Who would appreciate a hot meal more—a guy who just polished off a super-sized dinner or a guy on the street who hasn't eaten for days? The answer is obvious. By the same token, which person would appreciate being tossed a life preserver—the one standing onshore or the one drowning in the surf? Again, it's obvious. The ones who know they are in need of help are the ones who most appreciate it.

Now consider the two criminals nailed to the crosses on either side of Jesus. Both are being executed because they are guilty of serious crimes. Which one of these men appreciates Jesus's forgiveness? One man, despite being put to death, is still arrogant, and he dismisses and mocks Jesus. The other man knows he's being executed because he's a criminal, but he also knows who Jesus is. He understands that Jesus is the Son of God, and he respects that Jesus has the power to forgive sin. He's the man who knows he's in need, and he's the man Jesus promises to take to paradise with him.

Can you imagine how amazed the thief must have been in that moment? What had started out as a dark day suddenly turned promising—he received a second chance and an invitation to a brand-new life. All because he knew that he was a sinner and that Jesus was a forgiver—he understood that he had a need Jesus could meet.

How do you respond to Jesus's grace? Do you see your need of forgiveness? Do you welcome God's mercy like the guy on the cross did? Or do you think you're such a good person you don't need it?

My Prayer

Dear God,
I'm so thankful for your mercy and forgiveness. Help me to always be amazed by your grace toward me. I never want to take it for granted or push it away.
Amen.

Stone
for the Journey

I need God's grace 24-7.

Final Word

His Spirit lets us know that together with Christ we will be given what God has promised. We will also share in the glory of Christ, because we have suffered with him.

Romans 8:17 CEV

80

Unity

Words from the Rock

I am not praying just for these followers. I am also praying for everyone else who will have faith because of what my followers will say about me. I want all of them to be one with each other, just as I am one with you and you are one with me. I also want them to be one with us. Then the people of this world will believe that you sent me.

John 17:20–21 CEV

Jesus had you specifically in mind when he prayed these words. He knew that generations of believers would come and go for ages and ages—and he knew that you would be one of them. As hard as it is to wrap your mind around this, nearly two thousand years before you were born, *Jesus prayed for you*. What was the focus of this prayer? Jesus's heartfelt request was that God would make his believers one. He wants us to be united, joined together in heart and purpose, bound together in love. Jesus wants his followers to be connected to each other the same way he is connected to his Father.

Is that what you observe when you look at Christians today? Do you sense a strong bond of oneness between different churches and denominations? Do the Baptists love the Presbyterians? Do the Methodists love the Lutherans? If these questions make you stop to wonder, you're not alone. Unfortunately, reports of church disputes, theological bickering, and Christians arguing among themselves tend to circulate. When outsiders hear these stories, they feel repulsed. Who wants to become part of a group that claims to love one another but treats each other like enemies? Isn't that a little hypocritical? And don't you think it must break Jesus's heart?

So what's your responsibility? Do you do your part in helping the Christian community to be united in love? Do you do your best to promote oneness? Do you love your Christian brothers and sisters? Jesus prayed that you would be one with fellow believers, but he knows you have a choice in the matter. He prays that you will choose love. How do you pray?

My Prayer

Dear God,
I want to echo Jesus's prayer—that all Christian believers would be one. Please show me how to help make this happen. Let your love flow through me.
Amen.

Stone
for the Journey

God wants me to promote unity.

Final Word

Whoever loves his brother lives in the light, and there is nothing in him to make him stumble.

1 John 2:10 NIV

Reputation

81

Words from the Rock

I have given them the glory you gave me, so they may be one as we are one. I am in them and you are in me. May they experience such perfect unity that the world will know that you sent me and that you love them as much as you love me.

John 17:22–23 NLT

*I*magine that you just arrived in a new town and you're really hungry. You spot a nice-looking restaurant with a brightly lit sign that says, "Delicious Food Served Here." Okay, no one needs to twist your arm. But you're barely inside when a foul odor hits you. You glance in the kitchen and see the cook pick a hamburger off the floor and slap it on a plate. The waitress, wearing a stained apron, makes a hacking cough as she points you to a dirty table. Then suddenly a green-faced guy leaves his half-eaten meal behind, and as he races for the bathroom, he hurls right there on the filthy linoleum floor. Still hungry?

What if that's how nonbelievers feel about the church? What if someone is spiritually hungry and sees a cheerful sign that lures him into some kind of fellowship group, but once he's inside, he observes bickering and fighting and hatred and jealousy? Would he stick around? Or would he have raced (like you would have from the creepy restaurant) in the opposite direction?

Jesus knows that when his followers truly love each other, it naturally draws outsiders in. Believers who forgive each other, practice kindness, and want to help others can attract a positive kind of attention that reflects well on Jesus. In other words, people recognize that Jesus is loving and forgiving when believers practice love and forgiveness on a regular basis. His reputation is established by us. It seems simple enough, but sometimes Christians lose sight of this.

What kind of reputation are you giving Jesus? What do others see when they look at you?

My Prayer

Dear God,
I want to reflect your goodness by the way I live. I want my actions to point others toward you. Please show me practical ways to express your love.
Amen.

Stone
for the Journey

**God's love
is reflected
in me.**

Final Word

May you always be filled with the fruit of your salvation—the righteous character produced in your life by Jesus Christ—for this will bring much glory and praise to God.

Philippians 1:11 NLT

82

Heavenly Hopes

Words from the Rock

Father, I want everyone you have given me to be with me, wherever I am. Then they will see the glory that you have given me, because you loved me before the world was created.

John 17:24 CEV

What if you were just going about your day with nothing much to do because it's a Saturday, and you're broke, so you don't have any plans? You pass by this new amusement park, which is supposed to be awesome, and you see that they're running a special introductory offer—free admission, free rides, and even free food for a limited time only. What would you do? If you're like most people, you'd go inside, get on your phone, and call your best friends to come join you, because something that great needs to be shared!

Maybe that's a tiny bit how Jesus feels as he prays this prayer. He's asking his Father to make sure all his followers will join him in heaven. Jesus is still on earth when he makes this request, and it's been a while since he was in heaven. But he knows heaven well since he was with his Father at the beginning of time and they created it together. Chances are he's been missing it. And because he knows how absolutely fabulous that kingdom is, he wants all his friends to enjoy the amazing experience with him!

Can you imagine Jesus's anticipation? It's not easy to envision heaven because it's so far outside the realm of our earthly experience, but Jesus must have been incredibly excited at the prospect of gathering all his friends around him in the most spectacular, most incredible, most wonderful place in the entire universe.

How do you feel when you think about heaven? Hopeful? Excited? Do you want to talk to others about heaven?

My Prayer

Dear God,
I admit that heaven boggles my mind. Please give me glimpses of how fantastic it will be so I can be as enthusiastic about your kingdom as you are.
Amen.

Stone
for the Journey

**Heaven
is beyond
my wildest
expectations.**

Final Word

Above all, you must live as citizens of heaven, conducting yourselves in a manner worthy of the Good News about Christ.

Philippians 1:27 NLT

83

Love Letter

Words from the Rock

Righteous Father, the world has never known you,
but I have known you, and these disciples know
that you sent me on this mission. I have made
your very being known to them—who you are and
what you do—and continue to make it known, so
that your love for me might be in them exactly as
I am in them.

John 17:25–26 Message

What if you really, really loved someone, but they lived in an extremely remote place on the other side of the planet—a location so removed that there was no internet and no phones, and it was too far for you to travel there? What if your only hope of communicating your love to them was through the postal service, which only delivered mail once in a while? Of course, you would write that person a letter. A very carefully worded letter in which you'd represent all of your thoughts, dreams, hopes, desires . . . and love for them. You would want to write the perfect love letter.

That's kind of how God felt—only his love letter came in the form of his Son. Jesus came to earth to express every loving thought, dream, hope, and desire that God has for you. All of this was written on Jesus's heart and delivered to earth so you could understand how much God loves you. A perfect love letter.

In the same way, Jesus wants you to be his love letter. You are the way that Jesus, now in heaven, can communicate with the people around you. Your kindness, your helpfulness, your caring, your generosity, your love . . . all convey the love that Jesus wants to share with others. You are his love letter.

My Prayer

Dear God,
Thank you for sending Jesus as your love letter.
Please help me to be a better message of love to the people around me.
Amen.

Stone
for the Journey

Jesus sends his love through me.

Final Word

If we can encourage others, we should encourage them. If we can give, we should be generous. If we are leaders, we should do our best. If we are good to others, we should do it cheerfully.

Romans 12:8 CEV

84

Caught by Surprise

Words from the Rock

> Jesus told [the soldiers], "I am Jesus!" At once they all backed away and fell to the ground. Jesus again asked, "Who are you looking for?"
>
> "We are looking for Jesus from Nazareth," they answered.
>
> This time Jesus replied, "I have already told you that I am Jesus. If I am the one you are looking for, let these others go. Then everything will happen, just as I said, 'I did not lose anyone you gave me.'"
>
> John 18:5–9 CEV

t's nighttime, and Judas (the betrayer) has just led the soldiers to an olive grove and pointed out Jesus. But for some reason the soldiers are confused. So Jesus loudly proclaims who he is, which results in the soldiers falling to the ground. Can you imagine this? An unarmed man simply tells them he is Jesus, and these armed and trained soldiers are suddenly tripping all over themselves, falling to the ground like little children. If Jesus had wanted to escape, this would have been the moment to do it.

Yet he remains and asks them (again) who they're looking for. Then he tells them (again) that he's their man. How much plainer can he make it? Still, they seem reluctant, as if they understand that Jesus is the real deal, and they'd rather not arrest him. But they must follow orders, given to them by the religious leaders who want to do away with Jesus—anything less could cost them their jobs.

Picture their shock when Jesus is willing to go with them. He makes no resistance. In a way, it's like he's saying, "Come on, let's get this over with." The soldiers must be stunned by all this. Perhaps, later on, after news of Jesus's death and resurrection circulates, they recall this night and how they fell to the ground . . . and perhaps they become believers too.

When Jesus reveals his identity, it can catch you by surprise. Hopefully it will change your life.

My Prayer

Dear God,
Thank you for Jesus's willingness to cooperate with the mission you gave him. Thank you for revealing who you are through him. I know that knowledge is changing my life.
Amen.

Stone
for the Journey

God's love sometimes catches me unaware.

Final Word

Do this, understanding the present time. The hour has come for you to wake up from your slumber, because our salvation is nearer now than when we first believed.

Romans 13:11 NIV

85

Spiritual War

Words from the Rock

*Simon Peter, who had a sword, drew it and struck
the high priest's servant, cutting off his right
ear. . . .*

> *Jesus commanded Peter, "Put your sword away!
Shall I not drink the cup the Father has given
me?"*

John 18:10–11 NIV

*I*t's a natural and noble response to want to defend someone
you love. But suppose you were a mouse and your friend was
a lion. How much sense would it make for you to put up your little
mouse dukes and attempt to defend your powerful friend? It's a nice
gesture but unnecessary. In a way, that was a bit like Peter trying to
defend Jesus. (Remember, Jesus is God's Son, and all power is his.)

There was even more at stake on this night. Jesus knew exactly
what was coming down, and he was ready for it. His battle wasn't
against these bumbling soldiers—he was launching a spiritual war

for the souls of all humankind. Jesus was engaging in a war that only he could fight and only he could win. For someone like Peter (who meant well) to interfere would only mess things up. It also showed that Peter was still thinking from his earthbound brain. He was still deluded in assuming that Jesus had come to rule and reign in an earthly way. Jesus's plan was much bigger than that.

Sometimes you may be like Peter—you get consumed in earthbound thinking. You forget that God is up to something much bigger than the here and now. It's easy to get caught up in petty battles, getting trapped into thinking it matters who wins. In reality, it's the battle going on inside of you that matters most. Is Jesus winning that battle? Is he ruling in your heart?

My Prayer

Dear God,
Thank you for going to war for me. I'm so glad you won. Help me to remember that earthly battles are seldom very important.
Amen.

Stone
for the Journey

**God's victory
is my victory.**

Final Word

Because we are united with Christ, we have received an inheritance from God, for he chose us in advance, and he makes everything work out according to his plan.

Ephesians 1:11 NLT

86

No Secrets

Words from the Rock

Everyone knows what I teach. I have preached regularly in the synagogues and the Temple, where the people gather. I have not spoken in secret. Why are you asking me this question? Ask those who heard me. They know what I said.

John 18:20–21 NLT

After Jesus's arrest, he is taken to the high priest and questioned. The point of the religious leaders' questions is to arrive at something they can actually charge him with—something worthy of execution. They want him dead, and the sooner the better, since the festivities for their biggest holiday (Passover) are about to begin.

When confronted, Jesus answers them honestly. He reminds them that he hasn't hidden anything from them. He's always been out in the open about everything. They know who he is. They know what he's taught. He has no secrets. Of course, this only aggravates them more.

The priests' biggest problem is that Jesus is guilty of nothing. Although the hypocritical religious leaders are guilty of all kinds of things, they still love the law and would never want to be accused of breaking it themselves. They must come up with some other way to get rid of Jesus. With news of his ministry growing, his numbers increasing daily, and so many gathered in Jerusalem to celebrate Passover, the priests fear Jesus is a real threat to their corrupt way of life.

As evil as these religious leaders sound, sometimes Christians are no different. How do we often react when we're caught doing something wrong? Don't we immediately try to dismiss or shove away whatever is attempting to reveal our embarrassment? Sometimes we even push Jesus away from us—we don't want him to come in and shine his light of truth on the mess we've made. We'd rather hide it. But there are no secrets with Jesus. Just as he makes himself known to you, he knows everything about you. Instead of blowing him off next time you mess up, why not fess up and tell him you're sorry.

My Prayer

Dear God,
Thank you for having no secrets from me. Help me to realize how silly it is for me to think I can keep anything from you.
Amen.

Stone
for the Journey

I will live honestly before God.

Final Word

God has now revealed to us his mysterious plan regarding Christ, a plan to fulfill his own good pleasure.

Ephesians 1:9 NLT

87

God's Plan

You are right in saying I am a king. In fact, for this reason I was born, and for this I came into the world, to testify to the truth. Everyone on the side of truth listens to me.

John 18:37 NIV

ime is running out, and the priests are feeling desperate. It's almost morning, and Passover is coming. As badly as they want him gone, they don't have the authority to execute Jesus, but they do have him where they want him—sort of. Mostly they just want this mess swept under the rug as quickly as possible, so they hand him over to the ruling Roman authority, a governor named Pilate. When Pilate asks what Jesus has been charged with, they admit they have nothing on him.

Pilate must have rolled his eyes at that. "Take him back," he tells them. Naturally they argue against that, convincing Pilate it's up to him to handle this. So he confronts Jesus, asking him what he's done to get the priests so fired up. He also asks Jesus if he's the king of the Jews. Jesus answers honestly, and Pilate must have been a bit taken aback by Jesus's response because finally he says he has nothing against Jesus. He tells the Jewish people that in honor of Passover tradition, he'd like to release Jesus.

Those present at this early hour, the ones who hear Pilate's offer, are obviously not Jesus's followers because, instead of approving Jesus's release, they demand that Pilate release a gang leader named Barabbas. Pilate's hands are tied.

But Jesus knows his fate is in his Father's hands. Things are playing out just as they've been planned since the beginning of time. And these are the plans that change lives. How have God's plans changed your life?

My Prayer

Dear God,
Thank you for your willingness to go to such extremes to show your love and your forgiveness for me. Help me to never take them for granted.
Amen.

Stone
for the Journey

I will not back down from God's plan for me.

Final Word

You will live a life that honors the Lord, and you will always please him by doing good deeds. You will come to know God even better.

Colossians 1:10 CEV

88

Forgiveness Road

Words from the Rock

> *If God had not given you the power, you couldn't do anything at all to me. But the one who handed me over to you did something even worse.*
>
> John 19:11 CEV

This statement is made to Pilate after Jesus has been brutally beaten, whipped nearly to death, ridiculed, and humiliated. Pilate is actually getting worried at this point. He knows Jesus doesn't deserve this treatment. He already begged the Jewish leaders to take Jesus back and deal with him themselves. But they told him Jesus had broken their laws when he said he was the Son of God. So now Pilate is perplexed. It's his job as governor to keep peace among the Jews, and they're demanding that a religious threat be put to death. Whether he likes it or not, Pilate seems to have no choice.

Jesus tries to assure Pilate that it's okay. Jesus knows that the governor is simply carrying out what God knew must happen. In a way, Jesus makes it easier for Pilate. He tells him that God is the one calling the shots here, and those who brought Jesus to Pilate are really the guilty ones. In fact, Jesus has been saying this all along. So Pilate gives in to the will of the Jewish leaders and allows Jesus to be crucified. But Pilate's heart is not in it. He knows Jesus is innocent.

It would be easy to judge Pilate. We could condemn him for giving in. But remember it was God's plan being carried out here. Jesus was destined to go to the cross—someone had to make that call. And it was hard for Pilate. In fact, we don't even know how this event might have changed his life later on down the line. When Jesus went to the cross to ensure forgiveness for all, he had Pilate in mind too.

No matter what you do or how wrong it might seem, Jesus's forgiveness is big enough to cover it. How does that make you want to respond?

My Prayer

Dear God,
Thank you for forgiving me for everything and anything. Because I love you, I don't want to abuse your forgiveness; I want to always appreciate it.
Amen.

Stone
for the Journey

God's mercy is bigger than my sin.

Final Word

If I gave everything I have to the poor and even sacrificed my body, I could boast about it; but if I didn't love others, I would have gained nothing.

1 Corinthians 13:3 NLT

Forgive and Forgive

89

Words from the Rock

"Peace to you. Just as the Father sent me, I send
you." Then [Jesus] took a deep breath and breathed
into them. "Receive the Holy Spirit. . . . If you for-
give someone's sins, they're gone for good. If you
don't forgive sins, what are you going to do with
them?"

John 20:21–23 Message

After Jesus suffers an excruciatingly painful death on the cross, he is quickly taken down (before the Sabbath) and laid to rest in a rich man's tomb. For three dark days, his disciples endure the most depressing and hopeless hours of all eternity. Not only is their best friend gone, but in their minds, the hope of the world and the Son of God is dead. As far as they know, they're next. And all for what? From what they can see . . . nothing.

Then, on the third day, *Jesus returns to life!* He appears to numerous friends and disciples, who are amazed and beside themselves with joy. He tells his followers to gather and wait for him to give them some last words of encouragement. When he shows up, he greets them and then breathes his Spirit into them—his Holy Spirit, the one he promised was coming. The one who will finish all that Jesus has begun.

Is it surprising that some of Jesus's last earthly words are telling us to forgive others? He had just died a brutal death in order to offer everyone forgiveness and a new relationship with God. Forgiveness is at the front of his mind . . . and rooted deeply in his heart.

Jesus knows that forgiveness is the only way humans can live together. First we desperately need forgiveness from God. Then we need forgiveness from each other. We need to pour out forgiveness with the same generosity that Jesus poured it out to us. As he said, what good will it do to hang on to someone else's sins? Follow his example and forgive freely!

My Prayer

Dear God,
Thank you for forgiving me even before I knew I needed to be forgiven. Help me to forgive others quickly, even if they don't know they've hurt me.
Amen.

Stone
for the Journey

Forgiveness changes me.

Final Word

If we live in the light, as God does, we share in life with each other. And the blood of his Son Jesus washes all our sins away.

1 John 1:7 CEV

90
Always!

I have been given all authority in heaven and on earth! Go to the people of all nations and make them my disciples. Baptize them in the name of the Father, the Son, and the Holy Spirit, and teach them to do everything I have told you. I will be with you always, even until the end of the world.

Matthew 28:18–20 CEV

This is Jesus's last earthly commandment to all his followers. While it seems almost overwhelming in its enormity, it's also empowering. Basically Jesus is asking you to follow the example of how he lived on earth—with the additional promise that all the power of heaven will be backing you.

You have Jesus and God and the Holy Spirit in your corner now— as well as all of Jesus's disciples and followers who are cheering you on from heaven. In fact, all of heaven is urging and encouraging you to be everything God wants you to be. And you can be assured that

God won't call you to do anything that's too difficult—he will equip you for whatever challenges come your way.

Perhaps the best part of this last word is Jesus's promise to be with you always—even until the end of this world. And always after that too. No one else can make and keep a promise like that. But Jesus can. Anytime you feel like you're alone, or that you've been betrayed or forgotten or hurt . . . Jesus is right there saying, "I am with you always, even until the end of time." That's a promise you can hold on to—always!

My Prayer

Dear God,
Thank you for your promise to always stick with me no matter what comes my way. Help me to never forget this promise and to cling to it when times are hard.
Amen.

> **Stone**
> *for the Journey*
>
> **Jesus is with me always.**

Final Word

We know that Jesus Christ the Son of God has come and has shown us the true God. And because of Jesus, we now belong to the true God who gives eternal life.

1 John 5:20 CEV

Melody Carlson is the award-winning author of around two hundred books, many of them for teens, including the Diary of a Teenage Girl series, the TrueColors series, and the Carter House Girls series. She and her husband met years ago while volunteering as Young Life counselors. Visit Melody's website at www.melodycarlson.com.

Want to know more about the words of Jesus?

Dig in to this 90-day devotional from bestselling author
MELODY CARLSON.